Mix Butter with Love

A Deluxe Gift Cookbook

Illustrated by Francis Hook

Joyce Landorf

Harvest House Publishers

Eugene, Oregon 97402

To My Darling Daughter-in-love,

Teresa Landorf

641.5

MIX BUTTER WITH LOVE

Copyright © 1974 Harvest House Publishers
Eugene, OR 97402

Library of Congress Catalogue Card Number 74-18857
ISBN 0-89081-313-2

Fourth Printing, January, 1982.

Printed in the United States of America.

Contents

CHAPTER ONE
The Letter

Dear Darling Daughter-In-Law,

It seems like only yesterday when I had that first conversation with our son about you. True, I didn't know it was you. I didn't know your name, where you lived, or what you looked like—but the subject was definitely you. I remember it clearly.

I'd spent most of the morning dividing my time between routine household chores and kidding our son, teasing him about his dating life, or rather, his *lack* of dating life. For months it had been a fun topic around our house.

He appeared, handsome and darling, on TV's *Dating Game;* even won the date, but stopped dating in what I considered the "prime" of life—right after the show!

I'd said untrue and unfounded things like, "If *only* you weren't so ugly." "Maybe it's your boring personality." And then hitting my favorite subject, "How am I ever going to have grandbabies if you don't start with dating and end up married?"

We went at it all morning, alternating between mock seriousness to out-and-out laughter until suddenly he became pensive and turned quiet. I knew then it was time to quit kidding.

He was sitting now, directly across the sink from me at our kitchen counter. It was while I finished drying some dishes that he mentioned you for the first time. "Mom," he said, "there are a lot of really cute girls around and I *am* looking for a cute and/or beautiful one. But I want a girl who's more than cute. Like . . . I mean . . . I want to tell some really neat looking girl what I found in Psalms today. Then, instead of her looking at me like I was spaced out or something, I'd love to hear her say, 'Wow! That's really neat. It goes with a verse in Isaiah I read yesterday.'

"Mom," he continued, "do you know how hard it is to *find* a girl like that?" His voice, I noticed, was touched with optimism and he gave me a rousing smile before he left the kitchen.

He had just told me about you.

Mechanically, I stood there redrying a very

dry dish and it seemed the right moment to pray this prayer:

Dear Lord, I don't know her name. I don't know where she lives. I don't know what she's doing this minute, but someday she'll be my daughter-in-law. Right now, by Your love, I will begin to love her. I will stockpile large deposits of love here in my heart so I'll have plenty on hand when we meet.

Take good care of her, Lord, and until You bring them together, give them both all the lessons, experiences and, yes, even sufferings that will produce growth. Develop them into the adults You want them to be.

Bring her to us in these next few years. I'm eager to be *that* girl's mother-in-law.

Amen.

From then on, Dear Daughter-In-Law, praying for you became a daily pattern.

Some months later our son came home from a Campus Life Staff training retreat. No, I take that back. He didn't *come* home—he *floated* home. In less than five minutes I heard your name for the first time.

When I met you weeks later, you didn't know that for me it was like meeting an old friend. I'd talked with the Lord so many times about you, I didn't need a get-acquainted time.

The Lord honored our son's prayer for a cute girl who really knew the Lord and you turned out to be better than we ever imagined!

Your beautiful face with those blue eyes and blond hair all add up to a beautiful outward picture. The Lord supplied the inner beauty, too, because you absolutely sparkle with God's joy.

Even before your engagement was announced I was quoted as saying, "I can hardly wait to be *that* girl's mother-in-law!" Now that I am, I want to be the very best.

God's perfect marriage arrangement is found early in Genesis 2:24 (KJV). He lays the plan down in three parts.

1. Man and woman LEAVE their parents.
2. Man and woman CLEAVE to each other.
3. Man and woman BECOME one.

It should not surprise us when our society is hard on mothers-in-law. I suspect the cruel jokes, unfair puns, and out-of-proportion caricatures started with hangups about the first part of God's plan. The "leaving" of children or the "letting go" of parents is difficult for many.

On *both* sides of the in-law issue we have criticism, complaining, and bitterness. I highly doubt that a disturbed relationship was what God had in mind for a marriage that works.

I don't want to be the apex for conflict in your lives so both my husband and I have actively engaged in helping our son to *leave* us. The door has never closed behind him, but we *did* see him to the door. I even helped him pack! The person who said, "You must hold your children with open arms," was wise.

As your parents-in-law, we are taking that responsibility seriously. So there are two lovely things we do each day that involve you both. We pray for you, and

our hearts, minds, and souls are *always* available to you.

Now that you have both left your parents and are married, you can get on with the "cleaving" and "becoming one" steps in God's plan.

There are many great mothers-in-law—they just don't get publicity. They're like the six o'clock news broadcasts—unless they're bad, you don't hear about them. Yet, every time I find a "bad" one, I'm sure to run across three or four great ones. And as one young wife described her mother-in-law, she said, "She's just fan—tastic!"

I've been doubly blessed by mothers-in-law. All the twenty-one years we've been married I've had two. They are just great. (My husband's parents divorced when he was young, and both remarried many years ago.)

I can honestly say my mothers-in-law have constantly showered us with loving, meaningful concern. They have spent considerable time, money, and effort on us and we are deeply grateful for the dear friendships we have with them.

"Friendship" may be the key to a growing relationship. Once children leave and marry, we parents *cannot* be parents, particularly in the discipline department —our role changes to friends.

Besides having two great mothers-in-law, I have the memory of my mother who was a loving and gifted mother-in-law to my husband. When she died a few years ago, my husband's heart understood my sorrow completely because he himself ached tremendously over our loss. She always referred to him (addressing Christmas cards, etc.) as, "My son, by love."

These lovely women in my life gave me positive guidelines on how to be a mother-in-law, but nowhere is there a clearer picture of what we should be to each other than in the Biblical account of Naomi and Ruth.

I used to get all teary-eyed about Ruth's beautiful spirit and particularly her sentence, "Don't make me leave you, for I want to go wherever you go, and to live wherever you live; your people shall be my people, and your God shall be my God" (Ruth 1:16, TLB). But that was *before* I was a mother-in-law. While it's true that Ruth was *some kind* of a terrific daughter-in-law, Naomi must have been *sensational* as a mother-in-law to have inspired Ruth's devotion and loyalty. It seems to me, too, their love was definitely a TWO-way street.

It's sad how society sees and accepts loving friendships between friends, brothers and sisters, husbands and wives, people and puppy dogs, but *not* between mothers and their in-law sons or daughters. They feel friendship is impossible with one's mother-in-law.

I'm grateful for the book of Ruth because it clearly describes a truly loving friendship between two women. It gives me a glimpse of what *can* be between us.

Naomi's love for both her daughters-in-law was beautiful and the part I found most revealing about this love was when Naomi tried to persuade both recently widowed daughters-in-law to return to their homeland. She gave them this loving blessing: "And may He bless you with another happy marriage" (Ruth 1:9 TLB).

Naomi understood the "leaving of mother and father" and she wanted them to leave. But her loving attitude came to the front when she added, "May He bless you with another happy marriage."

It was then, after her farewell speech, Naomi kissed the girls and as the Scripture relates, "they all broke down and cried" (Ruth 1:9 TLB).

In her book, GOD SPEAKS TO WOMEN TODAY, Eugenia Price writes, "There is no better test of a woman's spiritual health than that she love her son's wife as Naomi apparently loved both Ruth and Orpah. There is no better test of a woman's spiritual vigor than the returned love of her daughter-in-law. This may take years to happen in some cases, but it can happen. Love itself is never limited by the circumstances of a relationship because God, Himself, is never limited, except by a closed heart" (published by Zondervan, 1964).

So, to you, Darling Daughter-In-Law, I offer my open heart—it was opened before I met you and now that you belong to our son, it *remains open!*

Now, this "open heart" policy is risky business because we may have conflicts. But so what if we do? To be open is to be honest with our feelings. To be open is also to be vulnerable to risk and change. But then, that's how real loving and living go!

So we will be open, available, and willing to risk hurt, or even neglect, for we want our love to wear well over the next fifty years.

Today, as I thought of those fifty years out there, I prayed,

> Dear Lord, You *knew* how good it would be to finally meet her, to see her, to hear her marvelous laugh and giggle, to know of her deep love for You and for our son.
>
> She loves deeply, this precious one, and she is at once both angelic and human.
>
> She is developing and growing into an excellent wife on her own. Help me as I do my part in steering and cheering her in Your ways.
>
> The law says she is my daughter-in-law. Your love says she is my very own daughter. She is my daughter-in-love.
>
> Thank You, Lord, for her. Please keep our love elastic and beautifully flexible so it can grow, expand, and create with each passing day.
>
> Thank You, too, Lord, for giving me the awesome challenge of being a mother-in-law. Help me to be the best! The *very* best!
>
> Amen.

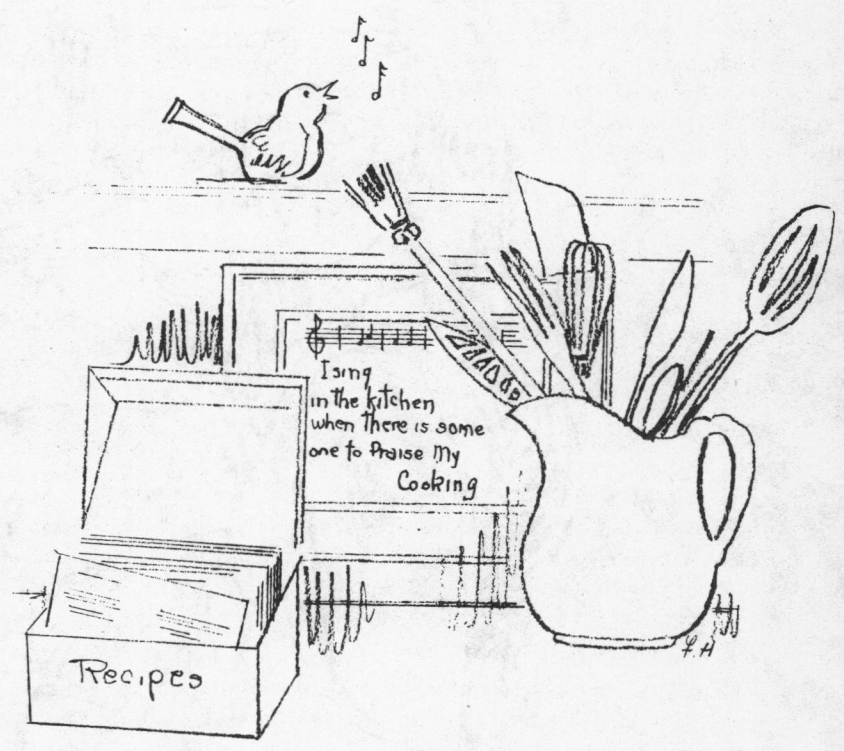

I sing in the kitchen when there is some one to Praise My Cooking

Recipes

9

CHAPTER TWO
Just One Request

Before you were engaged, and after you had eaten with us a few times, you came to me and said, "There is one thing I'd like from you." Do you remember what you asked? I do. You said, "I want all your really neat recipes!"

It's funny now, but that one small request started a train of thoughts zooming through my mind. Very soon you had me wishing I had a whole schoolroom filled with new brides just to give and to teach "some really neat recipes" to.

You had me fantasizing what fun it would be to share some of the practical *and* delicious joys of cooking. I could even see how helpful it might be to disclose some of my more eloquent disasters from the past.

I never started out to cook! The proof lies in the D minus I earned each semester in Home Economics!

During the first five years of marriage, when my D minus was put to work, I flopped and failed in everything from cakes to conversation!

Cooking was a bore. All I had to show for the hours of trying to cook was a cluttered, dirty kitchen. Actually, about the only positive thing I can remember about my cooking was that it was so bad we never put on weight.

Just the other day my mother-in-law was clearing the table after a dinner I'd cooked. She had already *told* me how terrific dinner had tasted, but as she reached the sink she said, to nobody in particular, "Just think, I remember when that girl couldn't boil water and even when she did, it tasted awful!"

I've given you this background because it seems in all of life if we have had a hard time with something, but have stuck with it, we usually become highly qualified to teach it. I think after my experiences I could teach *anybody* to cook!

Coming to Christ in the fifth year of our marriage not only changed our earthly and heavenly destiny, but every facet of living as well.

Asking God to be the center of our lives meant a thousand changes and the most significant change came in attitudes.

It's always surprising to me how much our attitude (good, bad, or indifferent) influences our everyday living. Take my attitude toward cooking, for instance. I used to go into my kitchen with D minus written across my forehead and mind. I'd stare at the stove (instead of a cookbook) and wonder why the stupid thing always double-crossed me. (Don't kid yourself—"a watched pot never boils" is not true! Mine not only boiled, it burned *as* I watched!)

The sink with the caulking peeling out of its seams and its worn chrome faucet served to remind me it was in cahoots with the stove. Whatever damage the stove maneuvered against my cooking, the sink would merely hold the great mess at the end of the day.

I faced every meal with this defeated attitude and it's no wonder mealtimes were occasions of high frustration.

When I became a Christian on that highly unforgettable day, it was my attitude in the kitchen that took the most astounding change. The idea that Christ lived in me and was there in my kitchen *with* me was at once both shocking and fantastic.

I knew before anything else happened I had to clean up the mess. Don't ever try to cook when counter space and stove are dirty or cluttered with used pots and leftover dishes. It doesn't seem to work too well.

The Lord has promised us "the sound mind of Christ" for our mental health. Then, for our physical well-being, we know He wants things done in an orderly fashion. Cleaning the kitchen was the first step for me.

No one, I repeat, *no one* begins by being a smashing gourmet cook, free from failures or setbacks. But I'll say this, a great cook does begin with a willing-to-learn attitude one step *outside* the kitchen.

After I'd cleaned (without a resentful thought) my kitchen that momentous day, I moved into the actual business of cooking the evening meal. I was tempted to go back over my past failures, but the new joyous attitude wouldn't let me. Instead, I asked for help.

"Dear Lord," I prayed, "I'm asking for a miracle, but only a semilarge one. Could You help me make something tonight for dinner that might taste reasonably good? I'm willing to read a recipe, listen to Mother, or whatever, but please help tonight's effort. Thank You. Oh, yes, one more thing, Lord, for me—keep it simple."

From that prayer to now, many years later, I've been cooking, failing, succeeding, and cooking again. It's been fun and a great experience since the Lord answered that last line of my prayer. Cooking, like clothing styles, is at its best when it's kept simple.

During seven years of broadcasting and doing my own radio show, I began to get recipes from listeners. I tried them all and saved the best. For years now I've been pulling recipes and ideas together and many are here in this book for you.

Some are the *very* ones you requested. Some I threw in for good measure. Most are fairly simple, use no fancy or intricate utensils, but taste amazingly good.

They will take a certain amount of concentration, time, and effort from you—so here we are, back again at attitude. However, if you take one recipe, mix with butter and a loving attitude, you're gonna be a smasheroo of a cook, Baby!

To start you off, here are some basic ideas that will begin to give you the joy of cooking. True, they are little things, but they're time-savers and creative tricks that go a long way in assisting you on your culinary journey.

Shortcuts and Helps

Keep a small shaker can of seasoned flour for coating chicken or fish; keep another with powdered sugar. It's great for sprinkling over applesauce, cakes, cookies or for jazzing up French toast.

Use kitchen shears instead of a knife for cutting marshmallows (you'll need to dip scissors in water from time to time), grapes, green onions, parsley, etc.

When green peppers, green onions, parsley, or what-have-you is on sale, buy it, chop it up, put it into a small jar, and freeze it. This speeds up meal preparation tremendously. You *can* buy these items already frozen in the market, but watch out for price. It's great to drop chopped green peppers into meat loaves or white cream sauces, etc., and, of course, frozen parsley can be dropped into *anything*.

Put your blender to work. It mixes dips, spreads, dressings, juices, frostings, etc. It shreds cabbage, chops nuts, and makes excellent smooth soup or cream sauces. Make *it* work for you.

Keep a small, wooden chopping board on the counter top for cutting cheese, meat, bread cubes, vegetables, or sandwiches.

When you're at school or working all day, avoid that rush to get dinner by using your pressure cooker, or, in the morning or night before, your crock pot, slow cooker, or whatever. In our time schedules, small appliances are valuable only if we put them to work.

Save steps by storing all cooking utensils near the preparation area. Keep an extra set of measuring cups and spoons near the stove, too.

Schedule your meals so the longest-cooking dish (probably the meat) is started first. You may want to slow-cook the main part all day or make it up to a "stop point" the night before. Then you'll pop it into the oven for twenty minutes to finish cooking and—presto—it's done. A sense of timing is very important in the kitchen and it takes a bit of doing (maybe years) to really get the hang of starting things, cooking them, and having them all finished at the same time.

My exasperated husband once said, "While you were sick, Joyce, I found I *could* cook a dinner. However, I *couldn't* get it all to the table at the same time!"

Your "cook-and-serve" ware will help cut down on cleanup. You should buy two small, inexpensive Teflon pans, one for just frying tacos, the other for bacon and eggs. Use the pans only for those specific items. Cleanup is a snap.

If you keep a bowl or pan of soapy water in the sink while you're fixing dinner, you can drop each used utensil into it for soaking and easy cleanup.

Have the man of your house keep those knives sharp. It's a time-saver for every job that requires cutting, slicing, or chopping.

If you peel potatoes or carrots, or grate cheese, do it over two sheets of paper toweling (even if you own a garbage disposal). They are easy to discard and the mess is gone in one swoop.

When serving guests or a big crowd, save time, steps, and energy by using a serving tray to serve the food and clear away dirty dishes later.

Speaking of trays . . . if you're serving "an after-church snack" to friends, use a large tray to hold all the makings for sandwiches, etc. Set your tray on a convenient counter or coffee table and let guests help themselves.

For your meals each night, just the two of you, don't use serving dishes. It only adds up at dishwashing time. Serve

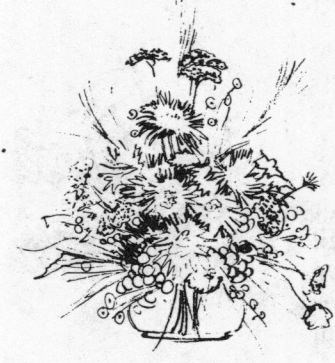

from the stove to your individual plates. As you arrange the food, you should have good color and design. (For instance, surround hamburger patties by bright wedges of tomatoes on each plate.) Using a green vegetable will always help the design and color of drab meat and potatoes.

One of the best ways to keep meals interesting is to keep the word "variety" in mind. Try crisp, crackly foods with soft, creamy ones. (Like icy celery sticks next to creamed tuna casserole.) Also use a bland flavored food next to a full-bodied flavor. (Like plain green beans beside very Italian spaghetti.) Change your pattern, too. Don't serve meat and potatoes *every* day. Vary your meals with main-dish salads or heavy soups once in awhile.

Try cooking at least one new thing each week. (You won't have a winner every time, but it will broaden your taste selection.) Learn to skim recipes in magazines, papers, and cookbooks with an eye for what you know are your tastes. Keep looking for new ideas.

Now a word or two about a pantry. KEEP ONE! Even if you don't have a deluxe walk-in closet for a pantry, set aside some place to store your food supplies. All you need are some sturdy shelves to hold canned goods. Don't store food in warm places above the stove or by the warm exhaust of the fridge.

When your grocery store has sales or

special buys on brand foods you like, buy two or three of the item. This not only saves money, but time as well.

Keep a small section in your pantry for "Gourmet Goodies." You may want to include:

Fancy canned french fried onions to top company casseroles.

Canned water chestnuts to slice into chicken soup or Chinese type foods.

Croutons for salads or casseroles.

Special ripe or green olives.

Packaged mixes like cheese sauces, dressings, gravies, or marinade mixes for meats.

Food coloring for frostings, dressings, etc.

Fancy canned fruit such as mandarin oranges, figs, or pie fillings.

One package of small birthday candles.

Paper muffin tin liners.

A box or two of muffin or cornbread mix to whip up for a "guest emergency."

Anything else that might add pizzazz to a meal.

Your weekly grocery shopping begins at home by checking your pantry and refrigerator. You can then plan at least your main dishes for the next week—before you leave the house. One other tip on going shopping—go on a full

stomach! Whenever I shop on an empty one, I buy twice the food I need. Besides, most of us are a little grumpy if we are hungry, so eat something before you go. I hate to run my basket into a grumpy lady.

Most cooks I know have a spice rack. Great cooks I know *use* the spices from the spice rack. The difference between "most" cooks and "great" cooks lies in the subtle use of spices. I say "subtle" because what you want to hear is, "My, what makes this so good?" Not, "Wow (cough, cough), you can really taste the curry in this, can't you!"

To me, spices come in two groups: main course or dessert.

Main course spices are:

Oregano Leaves

Use these for anything remotely Italian. A little bit crushed in the palm of your hand goes a long way.

Bay Leaves

Use 1/2 leaf in beef or chicken soups and stews. Good on pot roast, too.

Paprika

Use INSTEAD of bay leaves on the above. Use it too, for color on mashed or baked potatoes, warm breads, rolls and fish.

Rosemary

Use sparingly in chicken stew or dumplings. Good on fish, too, and great on "Fantastic Potatoes," (Chapter Five).

Dill Seed

See the fabulous recipe for "Herb Rolls" (in Chapter Five again).

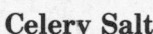

Ginger

Ginger loves soy sauce, but as a rule, you can use it in anything Hawaiian, ribs, chicken or vegetables.

Curry Powder

Curry powder loves tuna, so use it in "Hurry Tuna" (Chapter Three).

Celery Salt

Seasoning Salt

Garlic Salt

Sprinkle over vegetables while cooking. Use in soups, stews, or roasts. Sprinkle over sliced buttered rolls and heat under the broiler until hot and browned.

Dry Mustard

Use a pinch over baked chicken. Use one teaspoon in ham glazes.

Chicken or Beef Bouillon Cubes

These are the mainstay of good soups, stews and gravies. Use one cube to one cup of water or liquid.

Parmesan Cheese

This keeps best in your refrigerator. Use on Italian dishes—spaghetti, pastas—and vegetables like egg plant or zucchini squash.

Use as a topping on casseroles and breads.

This is also delicious sprinkled lightly over an oil and vinegar plain lettuce salad.

Dessert type spices might include:

Cinnamon (ground and in sticks)

Sprinkle lightly into the eggs for French toast. Cinnamon toast you know about, but it's great.

Also check the recipe for "Bo's Hot Tea" (Chapter Five).

Vanilla

Many recipes call for this well known flavoring so I'll leave you on your own here. However, Mark, the best man at your wedding, taught us to put one teaspoon of vanilla into the same eggs we put cinnamon into for French toast and we can hardly stand French toast any other way.

Allspice

When fall starts disappearing into winter, you'll need this spice for all the pumpkin pies you're going to bake.

Nutmeg

Use over a serving of canned applesauce. Also top a glass of eggnog with it.

I think nutmeg and butter over cooked carrot slices is different AND delicious.

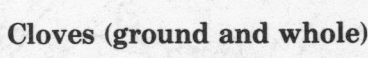

Cloves (ground and whole)

Use the whole ones to stud a ham (some year when you can afford a ham!).

Use ground in those pumpkin pies in November.

Of course there are many more spices and many, many more ways to use them, but this is your "starter" list.

I look forward to coming to your house someday and having *you* tell *me* what new things you've just done with such and such a spice!

Let's get on to the recipes!

CHAPTER THREE

Easy on the "Dough"

It's hardly a secret that in these early years your financial status isn't too great. But use this to develop your most creative cooking achievements. Some of my best ideas came when I had to "make do" with whatever we had (which wasn't much, let me tell you!).

Fortunately, I had a mother who drummed the "one dollar" idea into my head. Her philosophy was simply this: On week days, try to keep the cost of the evening's main dish meat to $1.00 for the two of you.

This has worked for years until the high cost of living shot that $1.00 figure out of range. But there are a few things left that can still qualify (prices subject to change while this book is being printed):

1) One pound hamburger
2) One pound fish
3) One large can tuna
4) One package smokies or sausages
5) One small chicken or chicken pieces
6) One small selection of cold cut meats
7) One pound bacon or cheese
8) One can corned beef
9) One large can of beans
10) Two or three pork chops
11) One pound liver (I know, HE hates it.)

So let's explore some of the possibilities from this dollar list.

1. One Pound of Hamburger

Baked Burgers

You need:
   1 pound hamburger shaped into patties
   1 can mushroom soup
   1/2 soup can of water
   1 small can sliced mushrooms (or several sliced fresh mushrooms)

With love:
   Brown patties in fry pan. Then place in a flat baking dish. Lightly salt and pepper them to taste. Put

soup, water and mushrooms into the fry pan. Stir and heat. Then pour over patties. Bake at 350° for 20 minutes.

Serves 2-4

These are good enough to serve for company. If you cook wide noodles for the starch of your meal, remember to spoon some of the delicious gravy over it. A green vegetable and a small fruit salad make this beautiful as well as delicious.

Hungarian Stuffed Cabbage

You need: 1 pound hamburger
   1 cup brown or white rice
   2 8-oz. cans tomato sauce
   1 chopped onion
   1 good-sized cabbage
   salt and pepper

With love: Half fill a large (4-quart) pan with water and heat to boiling. Drop whole cabbage into the water and let set for 10 minutes. Mix meat, rice, ONE can of tomato sauce, onion and salt and pepper. Remove cabbage from water (save the pan and water for cooking). Cut the core out of each leaf, fill with a small handful of mix and roll up the leaf. Tuck ends in with your finger. Place carefully into the pan of water. Add whatever you have left over (cabbage or meat) on top of the rolled cabbages and add the other can of tomato sauce. Simmer for 1 1/2 hours.

Serves 4-5

Stuffed Green Peppers Sublime

You need: All the ingredients for Hungarian Stuffed Cabbage but substitute green peppers for the cabbage. Fill peppers with meat mixture and cook with water and tomato sauce for 1 1/2 hours.

Serves 4-5

I was raised in Michigan and remember the winter months for the bleak, cold wind, scattered snow flurries, and something simmering on the back of the stove. The stove I remember best was my Hungarian grandmother's because she always had a large pot of stuffed cabbages or stuffed green peppers simmering fragrantly on a back burner.

My grandmother spoke Hungarian too rapidly for me to catch all she said so it was my Aunt Grace who taught me these recipes. Incidentally, these recipes taste even better the next day.

You should serve them both with plenty of thick sliced bread and top your cabbage rolls or green peppers with a scoop of sour cream—then you'll be a real Hungarian!

Six Layer Dinner

You need: A large rectangular, buttered baking dish. Then layer . . .

With love, all these ingredients, one on top of the other:

(1) 2 or 3 peeled, sliced raw potatoes

(2) 1/2 cup each of chopped green pepper and onion

(3) 3/4 cup uncooked rice (brown or white)

(4) 2 or 3 sliced raw carrots

(5) Crumple over the whole thing one pound of hamburger.

(6) Pour over one 8-oz. can tomato sauce.

Add one tomato sauce can of water. Cover and bake 1 1/2 hours at 350°.

Serves 4-6

I once spoke at a mother and daughter banquet in California and this Six Layer Dish was served as the main course. Harriet Vincent made it so I got the recipe from her. We've made it ever since. It does make a rather large casserole so you may want to layer it into two small casseroles. Bake one and freeze the other for later use.

This next recipe doesn't use hamburger meat, but the two beef shanks you do use are $1.00 or less in cost. It's a hearty soup made in the Hungarian tradition.

Grandma's Beef Soup

You need:
2 beef shanks
2 potatoes peeled and sliced
4 carrots peeled and sliced
1 onion peeled and sliced
2 stalks celery sliced (and some tops)
1/4 cup barley (if you have it)
4 beef bouillon cubes
4 cups water

With love: Heat water to boiling in a 4-6 quart

pan. **Drop beef shanks and four bouillon cubes in and turn the heat to medium. Cook for one hour. Add potatoes, carrots, onion, celery, barley and simmer for at least one more hour. (If you use your crock pot or slow cooker, just put the whole thing together at one time and let it cook all day.)**

Serves 4

This is best served with plenty of bread and butter.

Marion's Meat Loaf

Nobody ever made meat loaf like my mother! It was always savory, juicy, and just plain delicious.

Many times a dry meat loaf tastes like it's been mixed with seasoned sawdust. The difference in my mother's was one small can of tomato sauce and NO fillers such as oatmeal, bread crumbs or eggs.

You need: **1 pound hamburger**
1 small chopped onion
1 small handful chopped green peppers (if you have them)
1 8-oz. can tomato sauce
salt and pepper to taste

With love: **Mix ingredients together, place in a loaf pan, and bake 1 hour at 350°.**

While your main meat dish bakes, take advantage of the oven and bake potatoes or vegetables along with it.

If you do bake potatoes along with this meat loaf, don't fall into the "foil fad." Wrap-

ping potatoes in foil wilts the skin and *steams* rather than *bakes* the potato. Invest in four or five aluminum nails and "nail" each potato. It speeds baking and prevents a potato from blowing up all over your oven as they occasionally do.

One of your new grandmothers-in-law, Mildred, was thinking "practical and good" when she gave me this recipe for you. She knows, too, how much you both like Mexican food, so here it is.

Taco Pie

You need: **1 package refrigerator crescent rolls**
1 pound hamburger
1 package Schilling Taco Mix
1/3 cup sliced green stuffed olives
1/4 cup water
6 slices American cheese
1 package corn chips
1 cup sour cream

With love: **Brown meat and drain grease. Add taco mix, water and olives. Simmer five minutes. Place crescent rolls flat in the bottom of a 9″ pie pan for a crust. Cover with a layer of corn chips. Top with meat mixture. Spread sour cream over meat. Place sliced cheese over top. Add more corn chips and bake 30 minutes at 375°. Garnish with shredded lettuce, tomatoes or avocado slices.**

Vernie Patterson gave me a recipe for one pound of hamburger some years ago. If you use instant mashed potatoes, it's a real delicious quickie!

Shepherd's Pie

You need:
- 1 pound hamburger
- 1 chopped onion
  - salt and pepper
- 1 can string green beans
- 5-6 mashed potatoes or 5 cups prepared instant mashed potatoes
- 1 can tomato soup (undiluted)

With love: **Fry hamburger, onion, salt and pepper until meat is browned. Put meat mixture on the bottom of a 9″ x 13″ baking dish. Drain green beans and then spread them over meat. Spread tomato soup over that and add the mashed potatoes over the top. Bake uncovered 30 minutes at 350° (potatoes should be nicely browned by then).**

This next recipe is a departure from the "dollar idea" because you can't buy a roast for a dollar ANYWHERE. But I want you to have this method for roasts.

The beef roasts you've had at our house on Sundays come from a common recipe found in books, magazines, and newspapers. However, some time ago Selma Paulson, a friend and terrific mother-in-law, gave me her "how's" of doing it.

Selma's Sunday Roast

You need: A 4-5 pound beef roast (round bone, seven bone, clod, rump—it doesn't seem to matter)
- 1 package dry onion soup mix
- 1 can mushroom soup (undiluted)

With love: **Put the onion mix and mushroom soup over the top of the roast. Bake as Selma does in a covered heavy baking pan or as I do in one of those new-fangled plastic baking bags. It makes its own FANTASTIC gravy. Selma's way takes 3 hours at 300°. My bag takes 2 1/2 hours at 325°.**

Before Sunday school throw this all together and, if you're not running late, add two or three whole peeled potatoes and some carrots or green beans. Let it bake while you're gone and it will be ready whenever the preacher finishes his sermon.

2. One Pound of Fish

Here is a delightful way to serve any fish fillets. You could use Haddock, Turbot, Halibut, or any white fish.

Tempura Fillets

You need:
- 1 pound fish fillets or about 4 nice pieces.
  - vegetable oil for deep-fat frying
- 1 bottle soy sauce
- 1 box Japanese Tempura Batter Mix. (I get mine at the grocery store in the little section that has Chinese and Japanese foods.) I've tried making my

own tempura batter and *something* is never quite right.

With love:

Heat oil in your electric skillet or fry pan to 350°-375°. Whip up one small bowl of batter using box directions. Set aside in the refrigerator to keep chilled. Cut fillets into small pieces for ease of handling. Coat fillets lightly with flour. (The success of tempura depends on icy cold batter and very hot oil.) Dip floured fish into batter and fry in hot oil. Cook only a few minutes on each side using tongs. (Batter will be crisp but not brown. Fish will flake easily with a fork.) Place fish on a warm platter covered with paper toweling to absorb oil and set in warm oven. Serve with a small side dish of soy sauce (add a few drops of water to the soy sauce if it's too strong). Dip fish into it and ENJOY!

By the way, different vegetables can be dipped in the batter and fried the same way. Some of our favorites are carrot and celery sticks, sliced eggplant, cauliflower, sliced zucchini squash or long fresh green beans. The vegetables are cooked (but not to death) so they taste full of flavor.

3. One Large Can of Tuna

There are several million ways to go with tuna casseroles so I'll let you go reading on your own. Tuna loves a casserole so find a recipe you both enjoy. Here's a tuna top-of-the-stove casserole to get you started. It's a great one for that dinner where everything has gone wrong all day. It's almost impossible to wreck this one so it might be the only bright spot in your day.

Hurry Tuna, Please

You need:
1 large 12 1/2-oz. can white or light meat tuna, drained
2 tablespoons vegetable oil
1 apple, cored and chopped
1 small chopped onion
1/2 teaspoon curry
3 tablespoons flour
1/2 cup milk
1 cup chicken bouillon (that's one cube of bouillon in one cup of water)

With love: Fry the apple and onion in a little oil until lightly cooked. Add flour and slowly stir in milk and bouillon. That will make a lumpy white sauce. (The lumps are from the apple and onions and are not your fault.) Add tuna, breaking it up well, and sprinkle in the curry. Mix well. Serve over hot noodles which take nine minutes to cook and should have been started back while the apples and onions were cooking. If time is not a problem, serve this over rice. (Now that should have been started BEFORE the apples and onions.)

Tuna Patties

You need:

    1 large 12 1/2-oz. can tuna
    2 eggs
    1/2 small onion, chopped
      parsley
    1 tablespoon vegetable oil

With love:

Mix all ingredients except oil in a bowl and drop by a large tablespoon into a lightly oiled fry pan. Brown on both sides 4-6 minutes.

Serves 3-4

4. One Package of Smokies or Sausages

(I use Oscar Mayer Smokie Link Sausages—they seem to be a combination of hot dogs, sausage and ham. They also come with cheese.)

Smokie Casserole

You need:

    1 package Smokies
    1 package Kraft Macaroni and
      Cheese Dinner
    1 can onion rings

With love:

Make the macaroni as Kraft directs. Place in a buttered casserole baking dish. Add sliced Smokies on top or push some down into the macaroni. Bake in the oven 10 minutes at 350°. Then top with canned onion rings and bake 5 minutes more.

Serves 3-4

Smokie Broil

You need: 1 package Smokies
                 10 little strips of cheddar cheese

With love: Slice into a Smokie lengthwise. Insert a strip of cheese. Broil for as long as it takes to brown the Smokie and melt the cheese (just minutes). This is the fastest recipe in the West!

Lazy Brunch

You need:

Your best waffle recipe
  1 package link-type sausages
1/2 cup chopped pecans

With love: Make your batter for waffles and after you pour it on the waffle iron, sprinkle with chopped pecans. Meanwhile, fry sausages very slowly with 2 tablespoons of water. Cover for the first 5 minutes on low heat. Then remove cover, turn heat to medium-high and brown.

There is a marvelous maple syrup recipe in Chapter Five for your waffles or you can use jam. Serve with fresh orange or peach slices (depending on what's in season) to the side, and enjoy a lazy brunch.

5. One Small Chicken or Chicken Pieces
Chicken Basic

You need: A small whole chicken. Wash and place in a large 4-quart pan. Cover with cold water and heat. When it's almost boiling, add these ingredients.

With love:

2 or 3 sliced carrots
2 or 3 stalks sliced celery
handful of leafy celery tops
(I don't *know* why, but my grandma said chicken soups or stews must *always* have celery tops in them.)
3 chicken bouillon cubes
1 teaspoon of salt
pepper to taste
1/2 bay leaf (to be fished out later)
1/4 cup uncooked rice

After it boils, turn it down and let simmer for two hours or most of the morning—whichever comes first. Set aside to cool. Carefully remove chicken (and bay leaf and celery tops if you can find them. Cut the entire chicken up into bite-size pieces.

Now you have a large pot of basic stock liquid and a bowl of chicken meat with which you can do many things. Here are three ideas.

Chicken Soup

Use the basic stock liquid and add chicken (or half) and heat.

Serves 6

Chicken 'n Dumplings

Use the basic stock liquid with all the chicken meat and make the dumpling recipe exactly as it is on the back of the Bisquick box.

Cook dumplings 10 minutes without covering and 10 minutes with a cover.

Just before you serve it, sprinkle fresh or frozen chopped parsley over the dumplings. Be prepared for a lot of "ooh's and ah's."

Serves 4

Banquet Chicken or Creamed Something Over Baked Something

You need:

2 cups chicken meat
3 tablespoons butter
3 tablespoons flour
salt and pepper to taste
2 cups milk
1 cup basic chicken stock liquid
1 10-oz. package frozen peas or broccoli (cooked)

With love: Make a white cream sauce by beating butter slowly until melted, then adding flour, salt, and pepper. Stir with that wire whip you got as a shower gift. Add milk VERY slowly. This helps prevent lumps. Cook slowly—wait for it to thicken. Then add chicken stock, cooked drained vegetables and chicken meat, and continue to heat. Then make something for this to run over—biscuits, toast, mashed potatoes, rice or (when you want to go fancy) pre-baked pastry shells.

If you made Chicken Basic and used the soup idea and only half of the chicken, here is a recipe for that leftover half-a-bowl of meat.

Chicken Taquitos With Avocado Dip

You need:

> 1/2 bowl of cooked bite-size
>   chicken (or one big cupful)
> 1 package tortillas
> 1 can frozen avocado dip
>   oil for frying

With love:

> **Thaw dip and add a bit of mayonnaise and some chopped onions or tomatoes if you want. Keep chilled until dinner time. Heat oil in your taco fry pan. Swish each tortilla in and out of the hot oil just to soften it. Stack on a plate. On the center of each tortilla, lay a small handful of chicken. Roll it up and using tongs, put tortilla in the fry pan. Turn once to brown. Remove and place in a warm platter or basket.**

Serve taquitos and dip them into avocado dip with each bite.

Rick's Chicken

You need:

> 4 pieces chicken (or more)
> 1 small bag potato chips
> 1/2 cup melted butter
>   garlic salt

With love:

> **Tear a small air hole in the potato chip bag and then crush the chips**

with a rolling pin. Open the bag lengthwise with a knife, then sprinkle lightly with garlic salt. Dip pieces of chicken into melted butter and then into potato chips. Place chicken skin-side-up in a flat baking dish or cookie sheet. Bake uncovered one hour at 375°.

Serves 2

If you get elected to bring a casserole to a potluck supper sometime, here's a winner!

Super Chicken

You need: 1 1/2 cups raw brown or white rice
> 2 cans cream of mushroom (or chicken) soup
> 2 soup cans water
> 1 package dry onion soup mix
> 1 1/2 pounds chicken fryers or pieces
>   salt, pepper and paprika

With love: **Spread uncooked rice in baking dish and pour undiluted soup evenly over it. Add water. Sprinkle with dry soup mix. Salt and pepper chicken. Lay skin-side-up on the rice. Sprinkle lightly with paprika. Cover with lid or foil. Bake at 300° about 2 hours.**

Serves 6

Easy Barbecued Chicken

You need:

> 2-5 chicken pieces, placed in a plastic baking bag
>
> 1 small bottle ready-made barbecue sauce

With love:

> Simply empty bottle over chicken pieces, tie up the bag, poke air holes, and bake 1 hour at 350°.

6. Cold Cuts
Luncheon for the Girls

You need:

> To locate a delicatessen or meat market that sells an unusual selection of cold cuts and cheeses.

With love:

> Arrange meats on a large tray or fancy platter—like cotto salami, ham (chipped or sliced), or leftover beef roast slices. Combine with small blocks of cheddar cheese and half slices of Swiss cheese. Give it color by using small cherry tomatoes, green and black olives and dill pickle halves. Add a basket of hot rolls and individual bowls of green salad and you've got a different but delicious lunch.

7. One Pound of Bacon or Cheese

Never underestimate the power of a B.L.T. (bacon, lettuce and tomato sandwich). It's a big lunch time favorite and it's a nutritionally balanced meal all by itself.

If you want to use it as an evening meal, precede it with a heavy cream soup (tomato, potato, or mushroom). Follow with a substantial dessert (apple pie or German chocolate cake).

Quiche Lorraine

You need: A 9-inch pie crust (use packaged mix)

> 8 slices of bacon
>
> 3 eggs, beaten
>
> 1 3/4 cups half and half, if you have it, or milk (which you probably have)
>
> 2 cups shredded Swiss (or light cheddar) cheese
>
> salt and pepper to taste
>
> dash of nutmeg
>
> 1 tablespoon flour

With love: Make the pie crust as box directs. Line a pie pan with the crust and bake for *six minutes only* at 475°. Let cool. Reduce oven temperature to 325°. Cook bacon and crumble. Put bacon (set aside 2 tablespoons for later) into the bottom of pie crust. Combine rest of ingredients in a bowl. Beat with a wire whisk. Pour over bacon and crust. Sprinkle remaining 2 tablespoons of bacon on top. Bake in a slow oven at 325° for 35-40 minutes or till almost set in the center. Let it rest after it's out of the oven and cool 10 minutes before serving.

Serves 6

Eleanor's After Church Snack

You need:

    1 8-ounce jar Cheese Whiz Spread
    1/2 cup mayonnaise
    1 small can chopped olives
    3 or 4 strips of bacon that have been fried and crumbled
    hamburger buns or rolls

With love:

Mix all the ingredients together before you go to church. Then right after the service get home and spread it on hamburger buns. Broil these open-faced goodies until they are brown and bubbly. Serve immediately.

Serves 6-8

My Irish father is responsible for this recipe and even "cabbage haters" revise their opinion on cabbage after they've tasted this one. It's another one of those tastes-better-on-the-second-day recipes and keeps well refrigerated.

8. One Can of Corned Beef
Dad's Corned Beef and Cabbage

You need:

A large 4-quart pan, half filled with water; bring to a boil, then add
    2 or 3 peeled, sliced potatoes
    2 or 3 sliced carrots
    1 sliced onion
    2 stalks sliced celery
    salt and pepper to taste
Turn down heat and simmer for 1 hour.

With love: Add 1 cabbage (quartered) and 1 can of corned beef (break up the meat with a fork). Simmer 20 minutes more.

Serves 4 or more depending on how many vegetables you add.

Serve this with those little frozen packaged bread loaves and plenty of butter.

9. One Large Can of Beans
Best Beans

You need: 2 or 3 slices bacon
    1 tablespoon chopped green pepper
    1 small, chopped onion
    1 teaspoon mustard
    2 tablespoons maple syrup
    1 large (No. 2) can pork and beans

With love: Lightly fry bacon, green pepper, and onions. Add mustard, syrup, and beans. Heat until good and hot.

Chili Beans

With love: Top heated, canned chili beans with a hamburger patty, finely chopped onion, and grated cheddar cheese.

Serves 2

I don't know why, but this simple main dish tastes absolutely wonderful on a cold, rainy night.

Speaking of beans . . .

Beans 'n Berries

I'm counting on you to bring these beans to the family picnic on the Fourth of July, OK?

Don't let the unusual combination of ingredients discourage you from baking this bean dish.

It came to our house from Ruth Calkin who got it from a lady in the beauty shop who got it from her friend, etc., etc., but it's just delicious.

Make it and don't tell anyone what's in it until everyone tells you how good it tastes.

You need:

> **1-lb can regular cranberry sauce**
> **1-lb can regular pork and beans**

With love:

> **Mix ingredients together and bake uncovered in an 8″ by 8″ pan for 1 hour at 350°.**

> **Serves 4**

10. Two or Three Pork Chops
Stuffed Pork Chops

You need:

> **2-4 thick pork chops (Have the butcher slice a neat little pocket in them.)**

> **1 chopped apple**
> **1 chopped onion**
> **1/2 teaspoon sage**
> **salt and pepper**

With love: Combine all stuffing ingredients together and fill pork pockets. Place in a flat baking dish. Bake 1 hour (or until well browned) at 350°.

Baggie Pork Chops

You need: 2-4 pork chops, placed in a plastic cooking bag.
ADD

With love: 1 can chicken soup
> **1 dry onion soup mix**
> **1/2 cup water**

> **Be sure to poke holes in the bag. Then bake 1 hour at 325°.**

11. One Pound of Liver

Because many people hate liver, I've listed some helpful ways to enjoy it. Liver is valuable, nutritionally speaking, and can become a favorite—if given half a chance.

1. Thick, giant liver slices will NEVER taste good. The middle will be raw and unappetizing. Buy only the best thinly-sliced calf's liver.

2. Liver by itself is not too interesting. Start by frying a few strips of bacon and add one sliced onion. When they are lightly browned, remove and set aside.

3. Most people OVERCOOK liver and it turns into liver-colored rubber. After you've removed the bacon and onions, turn the heat on high (350° or 400°) and fry it on both sides in the bacon grease as quickly as possible. If you bought those beautifully thin slices, they will cook through immediately.

4. Two points against liver are it's shape and color. For extra pizzazz and taste, cover it with bacon slices and onion rings and place a small serving of tomato catsup next to it.

None of these wonderful directions have worked on our son, who still hates liver, but I've included these words in case you get hungry for it and he's out of town!

Now, let's get on to the salad department.

CHAPTER FOUR

Rabbits Aren't the Only Ones Who Like Lettuce

I wrote this title *before* I went grocery shopping yesterday and saw the high price of lettuce. So with apologies to Cesar Chavez, I think the title should read, "Rabbits Are Definitely The Only Ones Who Like Lettuce Because They Don't Have Any Idea How Much It Costs!"

Actually, today's high cost of lettuce (and most foodstuffs) has forced us to look at other types of greens. I'm finding "necessity is the mother of invention" and does a lot for creative cooking in the process.

A good salad begins by slipping the salad

plates or bowls into the refrigerator to chill. Don't ask me why salads taste better on cold plates, just do as you're told.

Since the price of spinach was exactly half that of lettuce in the produce department yesterday, I'll start with . . .

Spinach Salad

You need:

   1 bunch fresh spinach
   4 slices bacon
      Oil and vinegar dressing
      from a packaged mix.

With love:

   Wash, drain, dry and tear spinach into bite sizes. By drying it you'll help the dressing to stick. Then put it on "hold" in the fridge. Fry bacon rather crispy; cool and crumble into little pieces. (Try not to use those "bacon bits" found at the store. So far they haven't been able to make them taste any better than bacon-flavored cardboard.) Whip up the oil and vinegar packaged mix just before dinner. Serve chilled spinach on chilled plates. Top with dressing and sprinkle with bacon.

Tomato Shrimp Salad

From one of California's finest restaurants comes this simple idea for a rather glamorous salad.

You need:

   Several tomatoes. Plan to use this when tomatoes are in season and on sale or when your own plants are putting out a nice crop of tomatoes.
   1 can of tiny baby shrimp (or fresh frozen shrimp) chilled
      Oil and vinegar-type dressing
      Lettuce

With love: Arrange tomato slices on a bed of lettuce on individual plates. Sprinkle generously with shrimp. Cover each with oil and vinegar dressing.

Green Salads
(In General)

All I'll say about green salads is that usually they are ANYTHING green plus ANYTHING any other color.

You can have several types and colors of lettuce or salad greens, but even if you use only one green, it's really the goodies that *make* the salad.

Goodies like:

Radishes

Cucumbers

Green onions

Sliced hard-boiled eggs for topping

Thinly sliced and quartered salami

Black, green, or stuffed olives

Sliced fresh mushrooms

Raw cauliflowerets

Raw carrots curled, shredded, or sliced

Raw celery slices

Parmesan cheese for sprinkling lightly over the top

Small balls of cheddar cheese

Halved cherry tomatoes

Green pepper rings

Croutons

It would be better if you didn't use ALL these in one salad, but keep this list in mind, then check your refrigerator to see what's available.

Green salads don't always have to be mixed. You can take all those lovely ingredients and discover the Italian joy of antipasto —the ultimate in *un*-mixed salads!

Italiano Tray

You need: To simply dig out a beautiful glass serving tray (or any other large serving tray) and arrange (carefully) all those good munchy foods I've listed for green salads.

With love: Make carrot curls. Use a potato peeler to give you long, thin strips. Roll up strips and crowd, side by side, in a deep bowl. Cover with water and chill.

For celery branches, cut celery stalk into 3-inch lengths and make small slices on each end—not quite through to the middle. Place in bowl, cover with water and chill.
For radishes, make many "almost through" slices on the top. They will open after they've been placed in a bowl, covered with water and chilled.

(Carrots will curl, radishes will open, and celery will turn into miniature branches if, after they are cut, they are submerged into a bowl of cold water and refrigerated a few hours or overnight.)

Salami, Polish ham, or other cold cuts can be cut into halves or triangles. If you want to go fancy, soften cream cheese, fill and roll up a slice of meat. Secure with a toothpick and green olive.

Cherry tomatoes can be left whole and beautiful or you can cut off the very top of them and scoop out the insides. Then fill with tuna or deviled ham salad mix. For the added zing, use a little bit of horseradish in the tuna or ham. Dust the tops with parsley.

Olives, black and green, and green onions complete the Italian joy!
Top the whole tray off with little pieces of ice here and there to keep it all crisp and delicious.

Croutons

Some Saturday when you're a little bored, heat up about 1/2 cup olive oil and fry 4 or 5 slices of diced-up bread. Sprinkle lightly with garlic salt and Parmesan cheese and move the bread around while it browns. Cool the croutons on paper toweling. Store in a covered jar in the refrigerator.

Molded Jello

Now let's look at molded jello.

Here are some basic tips on jello:

With jello that's	use
red	Fruits of all kinds except fresh or frozen pineapple. Canned pineapple works fine.
dark red	Canned blueberries or cherries.
yellow/orange	Fruits, especially citrus and bananas. Vegetables like carrots or celery.
lime	Vegetables like shredded carrots or cabbage. Meats like ham, chicken or tuna. Recipes calling for mayonnaise or cottage cheese.

Use your kitchen shears to cut up marshmallows as a jello topping. It looks beautiful, especially on red jellos, and tastes great.

Here are some favorites of mine.

Strawberry Romance

(Great for Valentine's Day!)

You need:

1 large 6-ounce package strawberry jello
1 1/2 cups boiling water
2 packages of frozen strawberries
1 No. 2 can crushed pineapple
Chopped nuts
Small container sour cream

With love:

Completely dissolve strawberry jello in 1 1/2 cups boiling water. Add 2 packages of frozen strawberries, break up and stir until completely defrosted. Add No. 2 can of crushed pinapple and chopped nuts. Pour half of the mixture into a 9″ x 13″ Pyrex dish or ring mold. Jell. Spread one small container of sour cream over set mixture, then add remaining mixture on top and let set.
Serves 6-8

This next jello recipe, in fantastic orange, will look great on your blue and white salad plates.

Your first piece of furniture was an old buffet given to you by Eleanor and Roger Moore. We had so much fun stripping, sanding, and painting it! After we antiqued the hot Mexican yellow it turned out better than our wildest plans.

Well, Eleanor gave me this jello recipe and besides tasting delicious and looking great on your plates, it will blend VERY well with that old buffet! Orange is the most edible color in the world.

Sherbety–Orange Jello

You need:

- 1 large 6-oz. box orange jello
- 1 pint orange sherbet
- 1 small can mandarin oranges (drained but don't throw the liquid away)
- 1 1/2 cups boiling water
- 1/2 cup juice from canned oranges

With love:

Mix jello and boiling water to dissolve. Then add rest of the ingredients. Refrigerate and decorate top with whipped or dairy cream edging and a few orange slices.

Serves 4-5

I've never decided if this next jello is either a salad or dessert, so use it as the occasion demands. I first tasted it at Phyllis White's house during a fantastic sit-down dinner for 30 people. I've never been quite the same since.

The first time you ate it at our house your big blue eyes nearly danced out of your head as you shouted. "THIS I want!" (Right!)

Phyllis' Blueberry Deal

You need:

- 1 large 6-oz. package black cherry jello
- 1 15-oz. can blueberries packed in syrup
- 1 small can of crushed pineapple
- 1 cup chopped pecans (or walnuts)
- 1 3-ounce package of cream cheese (softened)
- 1 package of "Dream Whip" (prepared)

With love: Drain all the juice from the canned blueberries and pineapple into a one-quart measuring pitcher and add enough water to make 2 cups liquid. Set fruit aside. Heat the 2 cups liquid and pour into jello. Dissolve jello completely. Then stir in 2 cups cold water. Cool jello a bit. Then add blueberries, pineapple and nuts. Pour into a 9" x 13" dish. Place jello in the refrigerator to set. Prepare Dream Whip and beat in softened cream cheese. When jello is set, spread cream mix on top, covering jello.

Serves 6-8

Salads don't always have to be green or jello. They can be a complete main course.

Main Course Salad

Wait until we are having an unbearable heat wave. Then serve this icy main course salad with fresh rolls and plenty of iced tea. Top the dinner off with chilled butterscotch or chocolate fudge pudding. (Top butterscotch with a handful of chopped walnuts and chocolate with one marshmallow.) Eat it slowly and it will taste cool and you'll feel cooler.

You need: Any *one* of the following:

- 1 cup leftover cooked chicken, ham, roast beef or pork, OR
- 1 can tuna or salmon

1 can green beans, beets, or carrots, depending on how you want to go color-wise, OR use anything else in the crisper that looks interesting (lettuce, celery, tomatoes, olives) Thousand Island dressing (ready-made or mix your own)

With love: Mix all ingredients and chill. Add the dressing JUST before serving.

If you want to make your own dressing, here is a basic:

Thousand Island Dressing

You need: 2 parts mayonnaise
1 part chili sauce or ketchup
1 teaspoon sugar
2 small sweet pickles, diced

With love: Mix all ingredients together.

In serving any fruit salad, cole slaw, or Waldorf salad (that's the one with apple, celery, and nuts), here is a marvelous sweet dressing my mother made. It's light, sweet and VERY simple (but everyone asks for the recipe).

Sweet Dressing

You need: 2 parts mayonnaise
1 part maple syrup

With love: Mix both ingredients together.

My grandmother often served cucumbers as a side dish with lavish Hungarian dinners. You don't have to go to Grandma's house or be Hungarian to enjoy this refreshing recipe.

Grandma's Cucumbers

You need: 1 cucumber, peeled with both ends cut off
salt and pepper
a DROP or two of vinegar
1 teaspoon chopped green onion

With love: Use your potato peeler to peel off tissue paper-thin cucumber slices. Put the slices into a bowl and squeeze excess juice out of them. (This mangles the slices, but it's "important to get the water out," my grandma said.) After squeezing and draining, add salt and pepper and drop in vinegar. Refrigerate for an hour or so. Then squeeze them again—you'll get a little more liquid out. Just before serving, add sour cream and onion.

Before I close the chapter on salads, I want to give you one more recipe.

I called my Aunt Grace and asked her for her potato salad. NOBODY'S potato salad tastes as great as hers.

As it turns out, she is one of those born Hungarian cooks who doesn't read or use a recipe, but just sorta throws it all together. (*I* should be so fortunate!)

Even after I convinced her I was serious about wanting her recipe she couldn't imagine why I wanted anything so ordinary and simple. Further, she informed me, it was never written out and she didn't know HOW to write it down. I assured her I'd rewrite it properly so she wrote me a short note and included the recipe. (Honest, Auntie Grace, I planned on rewriting it, but you've done such a cute job—it sounds just like you —so I'm just going to copy your note.)

Auntie Grace's Potato Salad

She writes:

"*Well*, here's the potato salad. I just peel and dice up about five potatoes (raw). Then I boil them until they're tender and NOT TOO MUCH. Cool. Then besides potatoes I chop

> **3 hard-boiled eggs**
> **1 or 2 stalks of celery**
> **1/2 of a bell pepper**
> **2 tablespoons of dill pickle**
> **green onions or regular onion**
> **small amount of pimento**

Season to taste with:
> **Lawry's Seasoned Salt**
> **pepper**
> **red paprika**
> **parsley**

Then mix the whole thing up with *Best Foods Mayonnaise—HEAVY* **and good luck. (***Best Foods*** is the only brand she considers edible!)**

Serves 4-6

Love, Auntie"

Salads balance for nutritional needs. They add to the protein meat gives us, and the starch from noodles or rice. But besides that, salads give the sparkling color of jellos, the filling taste of main course salads, or the taste-setting flavor of side dish salads. Salads are fun! Happy creating, dear Daughter-In-Law.

CHAPTER FIVE
Vegetables and Froufrou!

Most people can leave their vegetables untouched and in tidy little piles on their plates. Other people, especially when they are in charge of cooking, think vegetables are the easiest to forget to cook. Experience has taught us how dreadful vegetables can be!

However, because of a creative mother and tight meat budget, I grew up LOVING vegetables. I hope some of the joy and enthusiasm I have toward vegetables will rework any negative thoughts or ancient prejudices you might have. After all, vegetables become *whatever* you *do* to them. Some must be dressed up elegantly in someone else's choice of clothes for they have little taste of their own. Others need absolutely nothing but basic treatments. However, *all* must be handled gently.

Vegetables, like fads, come and go. Right now broccoli is fashionable. (Peas are passé, and so it goes.) This chapter will include some vegetables high on the fad list and others that are good, but not "the" taste sensation for this year. All of them hold a special place at our table and I really feel they keep a dinner from being a dreadful bore.

Vegetables should be included in your diet because they explode with vitamins and minerals. They contain the nutrients needed for good health. Some vegetables like broccoli, peas, and spinach have vitamins A, B, and C, plus niacin and iron.

You need Vitamin A for healthy skin, for normal eyesight and for the "germ-resistant" factor in the linings of eyes, nose, throat and lungs.

Thiamine (or vitamin B1) is a vital factor in helping your digestion as you eat. It also assists in helping with the normal functioning of nervous tissue.

Riboflavin (B2) and niacin help in the metabolic processes of the body.

Vitamin C helps to keep connecting material between the cells in a healthy condition. One of the ways sailors in olden days knew they had scurvy, was when gums were easily bruised and bled profusely. Vitamin C also helps heal the throat tissues and your general health during a cold.

Iron (a mineral element) is present in the haemoglobin of the blood. It's vital in carrying oxygen to the cells of the body.

These are the hard core reasons for needing vegetables in our diet. I can't stress their importance enough. (As you can see, I'm a real champion for the cause of vegetables!)

The last part of this chapter deals in frou-frous which are the dimpled darlings of the dinner set. They give sparkle and fun; are extras that whisper "something special," and make cooking the creative experience it can be.

But for now, let's start with how to capture all the flavor of vegetables. Actually there are three basic ways to cook not only vegetables but everything:

The WET HEAT method—boiling, steaming, or anything using water.

The DRY HEAT—baking, barbecuing, broiling, or roasting.

And the FRY HEAT—sautéing, pan frying, or deep fat frying.

The Wet Heat Method

I didn't see one of those collapsible, stainless steel vegetable steamers among your shower or wedding gifts. So, if you haven't one by now—remind me. I'm good for one little steamer. A vegetable steamer is the best in the world for the "barely cooked" treatment of foods. Vegetables retain much of their vitamin and nutritional values because this method partially boils and partially steams the food QUICKLY.

Here are some vegetables and the approximate time for the wet heat method.

You need:

Fresh vegetables	Cooking time
cauliflower	whole, 25 minutes; flowerets, 15 minutes
broccoli	15-20 minutes
peas	8-10 minutes
green beans	20-30 minutes
corn	whole cobs, 6-8 minutes; cut corn, 5-8 minutes
spinach	3-5 minutes
asparagus	8-10 minutes
brussel sprouts	10-15 minutes
cabbage	10-15 minutes
carrots	whole, 20-25 minutes; sliced, 15-20 minutes
celery	10-15 minutes
artichokes	40-45 minutes

NOTE: If you are using frozen vegetables, simply cook as directed on the package and in the steamer.

With love:

Place your steamer in a sauce pan, add one inch of water, 1/2 teaspoon salt, and the vegetables. Cover and bring water to a boil. Then simmer until vegetables are JUST tender. Different vegetables will take longer cooking than others (see approximate time) and the only problem with this method is that you tend to lose the one inch of boiling water. (This week I ruined a perfectly good pan and the cauliflower because I got interested in the six o' clock news.)

Now, here are some ideas for some of these vegetables *after* you have cooked them with the wet heat method.

Cauliflower:

Whip up a package of Schilling's Cheese Sauce as directed. Then pour over cauliflower just before serving. Sprinkle lightly with caraway or celery seeds for fun.

Broccoli:

I love this best when it's in a chicken or ham casserole. But this goes down well with that same cheese sauce you used for cauliflower. Or you may want to get adventuresome and try your hand at a rich hollandaise sauce. (That comes in a package mix too, if you're too scared to try the "from scratch" method.) Try seasoning broccoli with 1/4 teaspoon of oregano.

You were pretty excited and tired at your rehearsal dinner, but you may remember these beans. I served them that night for all 30 of your wedding party and boys who "never eat vegetables" came back for seconds on "those beans." I didn't use fresh green beans, only canned, yet by simmering them in the bacon and onions they tasted like they were full of fresh flavor.

Green beans: Fry 3 or 4 strips of bacon and 1/2 chopped onion until both are lightly browned. Add cooked green beans and 1/2 cup of the water. Slice in 1/2 a can of water chestnuts and simmer all together for 20 minutes.

Carrots: Peg Bracken suggested, in her I HATE TO COOK BOOK (published by Crest), cooking carrots and potatoes together. She felt kids might take to carrots better if they were disguised, but I've found out kids aren't the only ones who like this combination! I wait for a particularly UNcolorful main course (like baked white fish fillets) and then I boil peeled and sliced carrots and potatoes TOGETHER. After they are cooked and drained, I mash them (together) adding a little milk, butter and salt and pepper. It's just delicious and it turns out a beautiful apricoty-orange blaze of color.

The Dry Heat Method

Some vegetables absolutely love being baked and respond by filling the whole house with the fragrance of loving, and they taste delicious in the bargain!

Here are some of those I-love-to-bake vegetables and their approximate baking times and temperatures.

Vegetables	Baking time
Baked beans	2 hours, or all day if you have a bean pot (350°)
Broccoli	*In* casseroles, for whatever time
Eggplant	25-30 minutes at 350°
White potatoes	1 hour at 400°
Sweet potatoes	1 hour at 375°
Spinach	(See "Ruth's Spinach For Company")
Acorn squash	30 minutes, cut side down, 10 minutes, cut side up, total of 40 minutes at 350°
Tomatoes	In a casserole or baked for 20 minutes at 350°

Here are some specific baking ideas and recipes for some of these vegetables.

Loaf Pan Eggplant

NOTE: Because of the meat in this it's really a main course recipe—not merely a vegetable.

You need: 1 medium-sized eggplant, sliced in 1/2″ slices (and you don't have to peel it)
Cooking oil
1 pound hamburger, shaped into patties
1 pound jar ready-made spaghetti sauce
1 8-oz. can mushrooms or 4 sliced fresh ones
1/2 cup grated Parmesan cheese
salt and pepper.

With love: Fry eggplant slices in cooking oil. (Add oil when necessary.) Remove eggplant and set aside while you cook hamburger patties. Using a meat loaf pan, stand eggplant slices upright and alternate with beef patties. Salt and pepper to taste. Pour over spaghetti sauce, mushrooms, and then top the whole thing with cheese. Bake uncovered 25 minutes at 350°.

Serves 4

Grandma Landorf's Eggplant Casserole

You need: 1 medium eggplant, peeled and cut into cubes
1 onion, chopped
2 slices bacon
2 egg yolks
1 teaspoon salt
1 cup bread or cracker crumbs
1/2 cup grated cheddar cheese

With love: Cook eggplant cubes in boiling water 15 minutes. While that's cooking, fry bacon and onion. Drain egg-plant and add to it bacon, onion, egg yolks, salt, and crumbs. Pour this into a greased casserole baking dish. Sprinkle cheese on top. Bake uncovered 40 minutes at 350°.

Fantastic Potatoes

You need: 4-6 medium potatoes, peeled and cut lengthwise into "fingers"
1/4 cup cooking oil
1/2 teaspoon rosemary
salt and pepper to taste
1/2 cup water
1/2 cup melted butter

With love: Fry potato fingers in oil until very lightly browned. Add rosemary, salt, pepper. Add water (slowly so you don't get burned by the sputter and spatter). Transfer the whole thing into a baking dish and pour over the top the 1/2 cup of melted butter. Bake, covered with a lid or tinfoil, for 40 minutes at 350° and uncovered for 10 more minutes.

Serves 4

Now—about spinach. I personally love frozen chopped spinach cooked the wet heat method and served with butter, salt, and pepper—PERIOD! However, at our house I stand alone on this so I've had to find other recipes that sufficiently disguise spinach. Here are two winners!

Your husband is one of the people from our house who hates (!) spinach, but one night at Ruth Calkin's home she served us baked spinach for the vegetable.

From the moment he tasted the spinach, his only conversation was about "GET-TING that recipe." (It's funny, I know Ruth is a terrific cook, but I can't remember one other thing we had to eat that night except this spinach.)

Ruth's Spinach for Company

You need: 1 small chopped onion
3 tablespoons butter
1 16-oz. can creamed corn
2 packages of frozen chopped spinach
1/2 cup cracker or bread crumbs
Parmesan cheese.

With love: Brown the onions lightly in butter and set aside. Cook spinach as directed and then, using a spoon, press the cooked spinach through a colander to drain all liquid out of it. It's important to get it as dry as possible. Then into a 9″ x 13″ greased baking dish mix onion, corn, and drained spinach. Sprinkle bread or cracker crumbs and Parmesan cheese on top. Bake covered 40 minutes at 300°.

Serves 4-6

Spinach Stuffed Manicotti

This is another main course dish—not merely a vegetable—and all you need with this is a green salad!

You need: 12 manicotti tubes (these are giant noodles to be filled with goodies.)

1 pound hamburger meat
1 10-ounce package frozen chopped spinach, cooked, drained and pressed
2 cups cottage cheese
2 eggs, beaten
2 tablespoons chopped onion
  salt and pepper to taste
  dash nutmeg (or 1/4 teaspoon)
2 8-oz. cans tomato sauce
1/4 cup Parmesan cheese

With love: Drop manicotti tubes carefully into boiling, salted water. (Use a large 6-quart pan.) Stir gently and cook for 6 minutes only. Drain and rinse with cold water. Set aside for stuffing later. Crumble hamburger meat into a fry pan and lightly brown. Then, into a large mixing bowl, combine meat, spinach, cottage cheese, eggs, and onions. Mix well. Add salt, pepper, and nutmeg to taste. Butter a large 9″ by 13″ baking dish (or two smaller ones) so the 12 tubes can lie side by side and close together in one layer. (Isn't that sweet?) Using your fingers (I've tried a spoon and it just makes a mess) fill the manicotti with the mixture and place them in the baking dish as they are filled. Pour 2 cans tomato sauce over the top and sprinkle with Parmesan cheese. Bake uncovered 25 minutes at 350°.

Serves 6

Baked Thanksgiving Squash

NOTE: You can serve this anytime it's in season, but it just smells like Thanksgiving when it's cooking so that's where the name came from.

You need: 2 acorn squash
  oil
  butter
  salt and pepper

With love: Wash and cut squash in half (either across or lengthwise—it doesn't matter). Pour a little oil on a flat baking pan (a cookie sheet will do) and bake cut side down 30 minutes at 350°. Then turn right side up, put a lump of butter in each one. Salt and pepper, and bake for 10 more minutes.

Serves 2 generously or 4 skimpily

I have tasted Southern Corn Pudding several times and it never did too much for me, but the other night I found out why. All the corn pudding I'd tasted had not been cooked by U.S. Army Chaplain Cross's wife, Virginia! Now SHE makes corn pudding! Here is her original recipe.

Virginia's Corn Pudding

You need: 2 eggs
1/2 cup sugar
1 teaspoon salt
2 tablespoons melted butter
1 16-ounce can cream style corn
  paprika

With love: Beat eggs well; add sugar, salt, butter, and corn. Pour into a 1 1/2-quart buttered casserole and sprinkle with paprika. Bake uncovered at

325° for 50 minutes or until it's set. Serve from the casserole.

Serves 4-6

The Fry Heat Method

This method develops the flavor of food. However, it is the best way to wreck your diet if you're watching your weight. I won't tempt you with too many "fry heat" recipes, but here are some goodies. Oh, yes, by the way, any cooking fat can be used, but butter (or margarine) burns quickly at high temperatures. So use butter for low temperature things like eggs. A vegetable oil is best for high temperature frying. I think you'll like the lightness of vegetable oils such as safflower, soy, corn, or a blend of these.

I've given you some recipes for vegetables that respond to the fry method and the approximate frying time for each.

Cooking time	Vegetables
Carrots	Cooked wet method 20 minutes, then fried 5-8 minutes
Celery	5-8 minutes
Bean sprouts	5 minutes
Eggplant	Deep fat fried 5 minutes

Vegetables	Cooking time
Mushrooms	2-4 minutes
Onions	5 minutes
Parsnips	Cooked wet method 15 minutes, fried 8 minutes
Zucchini squash	15 minutes

Here are some frying ways for a few of these vegetables.

Carrot Splendor

You need: 4-6 sliced and cooked carrots or 1 can of whole, sliced or shredded carrots. (I once bought a package of those whole frozen carrots. They simply NEVER cooked through, so they tasted rubbery to me. It wasn't too big of a disaster except that the guests for dinner that night were Bob and Shirley Hawkins—the publisher of this book!)
1/4 cup butter
1/2 cup (packed) brown sugar
1 teaspoon ginger
parsley

With love: Melt butter in fry pan. Add brown sugar, cooked and drained carrots, ginger, and sprinkle with parsley. Fry on low heat for 5-8 minutes, stirring often to coat carrots with the delicious glaze.

Oh, yes if you are out of brown sugar and ginger, substitute 1/2 cup of peach or apricot jam. It works surprisingly well, as I found out the other night.

Chinese Celery and Bean Sprouts

You need: 1 bunch celery, washed and cut into diagonal slices
1 good handful bean sprouts (either fresh or canned)
vegetable oil
soy sauce

With love: Do like the Chinese do and fry celery and bean sprouts in a little hot oil very quickly. Stir and lift the vegetables all the time (about 5 minutes maximum). Don't overcook because the celery and sprouts should be tender-crisp. Sprinkle lightly with soy sauce.

Serves 4

Side Dish Mushrooms

You need: 1/2 pound fresh mushrooms
1/2 cup butter

With love: Tenderly and QUICKLY wash mushrooms (you keep mushrooms

as dry as possible because a mushroom grower told me so!) then slice. Heat butter in a small fry pan and get it as hot as you can without burning it. Drop mushrooms in and stir. Fry for about 2 to 4 minutes.

Serves 4

(Mmmmm, this is one of my favorites, but the cost of mushrooms may be a regrettable factor.)

Zucchini With a Capital Z

You need: 4–6 zucchini, washed with a small vegetable brush. Dirt clings to this vegetable and can ruin every mouthful as it sandpapers your teeth, so scrub well.
2–3 slices of bacon
2 tablespoons chopped onion
1 fresh tomato or 4 cherry tomatoes

With love: Lightly fry bacon and onion until browned. Slice zucchini into pan and add sliced tomatoes. Salt and pepper to taste and fry on low heat until tender or about 15 minutes. (For an Italian twist, sprinkle on 1/4 teaspoon oregano before serving.)

Now for the froufrou!

Here are three breads that have flavor and pizzazz all distinctly their own. This first recipe has become a standard for any Italian type dinner we serve.

Maxine's Bread

You need:

    1 UNSLICED loaf of French
      bread
    1/2 cup mayonnaise
    1/2 cup butter
    1/2 teaspoon garlic salt
      Parmesan cheese
      paprika
      parsley

With love:

Slice loaf of bread lengthwise. Mix in a small bowl, the mayonnaise, butter, and garlic salt. Spread this mixture on both halves. Sprinkle Parmesan cheese, paprika and parsley on top. Bake UNCOVERED 10 minutes at 350°.

Herb Rolls

You need:

    1/4 cup butter (or margarine)
    1 1/2 teaspoons chopped parsley
    1/2 teaspoon dill seed
    3 tablespoons Parmesan cheese
    1 package refrigerator biscuits

With love:

Put butter, parsley, dill seed, and cheese into a metal 9″ pie pan. Stir and melt the mixture over low heat. Cut each biscuit into quarters and swish each piece in the butter mixture. Arrange pieces so they all touch. Bake uncovered 12–15 minutes at 425°.

Serves 4

Maui Honeymoon Rolls

You need: 1/2 cup (packed) brown sugar
    2 tablespoons flour
    3 tablespoons butter (or
      margarine)
    1 8 1/2-oz. can crushed
      pineapple, drained
    1/2 cup pecan halves (or walnuts)
    8 brown-and-serve rolls

With love: (and memories of your Hawaiian honeymoon) blend brown sugar and flour in a greased 8″ (metal) round cake or pie pan. Add butter, pineapple, and nuts. Heat over low heat until butter melts, stirring constantly. Place rolls, top side down, in the pineapple mixture. Bake uncovered 10-12 minutes at 400° or until rolls are golden brown. Remove from oven and invert onto a serving plate or tray.

Serves 8

Maple syrup has got to be one of the highest priced (per bottle) foodstuffs at the market. And unless you are buying PURE maple syrup (which is sky-high for a small bottle) all syrups are flavored with imitation maple flavoring. So why not make your own?

My Maple Syrup

You need: 1 cup white sugar
    1 cup (packed) brown sugar
    1 cup water

1/4 teaspoon maple flavoring
1/2 teaspoon vanilla extract

With love:

Mix both sugars and water in a small pan. Heat to boiling point and dissolve the sugars. Let it rest a minute or two and add maple and vanilla flavoring.

Makes 1 3/4 cups

Store leftover syrup in a covered glass jar or bottle. (Better yet, use an old store-bought maple syrup container.) The total cost of almost 16 ounces of home-made syrup is about 25¢ compared to 65¢ for the same amount of commercially sold syrup.

Here are some delightful things to drink. One is for summer and two are for winter.

Summer Cooler

You need:

Frozen lemonade, made as directed
ginger ale or creme soda pop
creme de menthe sherbet

With love:

Make lemonade and then mix in ginger ale and sherbet.

I didn't put the quantity down because you can make this for just the two of you or for a crowd. Use one of everything or several of everything and taste as you go along. If you make it for a crowd use your punch bowl and float an ice ring (freeze water in a round jello mold ring) and top with thin lemon slices. All this is surrounded by the sherbet and it's soft and cool in looks.

Every Christmas my friends Lila and Selma in Tacoma, Washington, go together and give a fabulous party for their church friends. Last year Lila casually mentioned the menu and just "knew" I'd love the punch recipe. She was right! I tried it and it's fantastic!

Lila's Christmas Party Eggnog

You need:
    1 quart ready-made eggnog
    1 pint vanilla ice cream
    2 cups 7-Up
    sprinkling of nutmeg

With love: **Mix it all up. If you get the job of fixing it for your Sunday school party, just quadruple the recipe.**

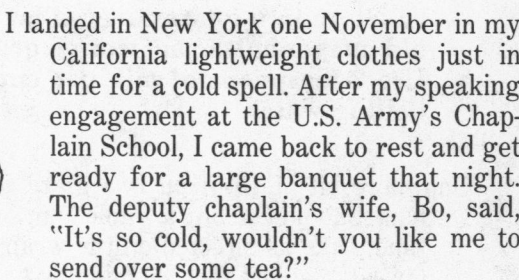

I landed in New York one November in my California lightweight clothes just in time for a cold spell. After my speaking engagement at the U.S. Army's Chaplain School, I came back to rest and get ready for a large banquet that night. The deputy chaplain's wife, Bo, said, "It's so cold, wouldn't you like me to send over some tea?"

"Oh, no," I answered. I just wanted to climb under some blankets, thaw out, and sleep a bit. But bless Bo's heart, she ignored me and sent her daughter over a few minutes later with a covered tray. That beautiful, hospitable gesture warmed me physically AND spiritually. The tray held a teapot of steaming tea, a dainty cup and saucer, and small dish of cookies. Everything was good but the tea was sensational!

Each time you serve it remember, since we *are* Christians, we are to be *hospitable* to others. You may never know how heart warming this tea may be to someone. Serve it with all your love.

Bo's Hot Spiced Tea

You need:

>2 cups Tang (orange drink mix)
>2 cups instant tea
>2 cups sugar
>1 small package Wyler's dry lemonade mix
>1 1/2 teaspoons cinnamon
>1 1/2 teaspoons ground cloves
>1 1/2 teaspoons allspice

With love:

>Mix all these dry ingredients together. Store in a quart covered jar (an old mayonnaise jar works great). Use 2 teaspoons of mix per cup of boiling water.

One more bit of froufrou is a glaze for a ham. Should you buy a whole ham sometime, bake as directed on the wrapping (or call me) and then 30 minutes before it's finished baking, spoon over HALF of this glaze.

Glaze Extraordinaire

You need:

>1 8-oz. jar peach, apricot or orange marmalade jam
>1/2 cup of honey
>2 cups of orange juice
>1 tablespoon mustard

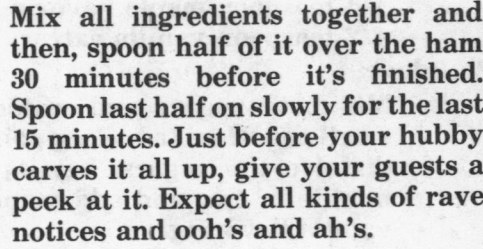

With love: Mix all ingredients together and then, spoon half of it over the ham 30 minutes before it's finished. Spoon last half on slowly for the last 15 minutes. Just before your hubby carves it all up, give your guests a peek at it. Expect all kinds of rave notices and ooh's and ah's.

About Coffee

Last, but by no means least, are a few words on coffee.

As you know, from hundreds of television commercials, if you can't make good coffee your whole marriage might blow up in your face (or so *they* would have you believe). Take it from me, marriages *do* break up over small, silly things, but a poor cup of coffee is rarely completely at fault.

However, we do live in a society and culture that suggests hospitality is connected to how well you make or serve a cup of coffee, so here are a couple of pointers.

If you can find a coffee grinder—grind your own. (It may be harder to find the whole coffee bean, but try.) Grinding it in your kitchen (as my mother *and* grandmother used to do) releases coffee flavor that's fresh and incredibly delicious.

Make your brew in a drip-type pot. Metal or glass container doesn't matter, but *don't* use a percolator-type pot. Percolating coffee is a nice way of saying, "Boil the soul out of it." The WATER should be boiled NOT the coffee. In the drip method the boiling water is passed gently over and through the drip grind coffee and what filters down is true coffee flavor with NO taste of bitterness.

Serve this kind of good coffee with one of the desserts in the next chapter and the "hostess with the mostess" won't have a thing on you.

CHAPTER SIX
Any Chance of Dessert Tonight?

Desserts are the festival time of any meal. They add a party flavor and make an occasion out of an ordinary meal so I've chosen the very best of my recipes and hope any time you make them they will accomplish their fun goals for you.

If you don't like to fuss with desserts, especially the make-from-scratch methods, we have enough ready-to-make dessert mixes on the grocery shelves to last 365 days without a single repeat. However, I am convinced we don't *need* a dessert every night.

I know one lady (whose entire family is watching their weight) who, when asked by her children, "What's for dessert?" names off every dessert from cakes to turnovers. Of course she doesn't have *any* of them on hand to serve. She merely tells them they are "available" (somewhere in the world). This is her way of coping with desserts she doesn't like to cook in the first place and are fattening in the second place.

Most of us don't need desserts, but it's VERY nice to please our sweet tooth once in awhile. So here are some words on sweetening up not only your tooth, but the dinner hour as well.

If you have served a heavy meal like roast, potatoes, and vegetable, or a "Sunday best type dinner," keep dessert light. A scoop of sherbet or ice cream, two kinds of grapes, and little cubes of cheddar cheese, jello, or a custard would be perfect.

If the meal has been light, such as a meat soup with bread or waffles and sausage, the sky's the limit on desserts. This is the time to serve that old-fashioned oatmeal cake or "One-Bowl Brownie Pie."

It has been said that a cake is the aristocrat of all desserts. So I'll start with some favorite cake recipes of mine. Some of them are the "scratch method" but others merely take a mix and go off the deep end. Like this first one.

Lemon Pound Cake

You need:
4 eggs
1 package (2-layer size) yellow cake mix
1 3-3/4-oz. package of INSTANT lemon pudding mix (dry)
3/4 cup water
1/3 cup vegetable oil
Lemon Glaze

With love: Beat eggs till thick and lemon colored. Add cake mix, pudding mix, water and oil. Beat 10 minutes at medium speed on electric mixer. Pour into ungreased 10" tube pan with removable bottom. Bake at 350° for 50 minutes. Leaving cake on pan bottom, remove sides of pan from hot cake. Using two-tined fork, prick holes in top of cake. Drizzle lemon glaze over top and spread on sides of cake. Cool completely; remove pan bottom. Garnish with thin slices of lemon.

Lemon Glaze: Heat 2 cups confectioners' sugar and 1/3 cup lemon juice to boiling.

Any time you split cake layers it always seems to impress people. (I don't KNOW why, other than it looks like you "cared" so much you worked your fingers to the bone.) So here are three recipes which call for splitting layers and filling with something. Save these cakes for the "boss's dinner" night or the impress-the-relatives dinner.

Fancy Walnut Torte

You need:
- 1 package (2-layer) spice cake mix
- 1 cup fine graham cracker crumbs
- 1 9-ounce container frozen whipped topping, thawed
- 1 cup applesauce
- 1/2 cup finely chopped walnuts

With love: Prepare cake mix according to package directions, adding graham cracker crumbs to mix before beating and bake in two greased and floured 9" layer pans. Split cooled layers to form 4 thin layers. Combine 1 cup of the whipped topping and the applesauce. Spread about 1/2 cup applesauce mixture on each of three layers and stack. Top with fourth layer. Frost sides and top with remaining whipped topping. Sprinkle with chopped walnuts. Chill 1 hour before serving. Store leftover cake in refrigerator.

"Highjacked" Chocolate Cake

(I've named it thus because on a flight from New York to California I was served this kind of cake. I "highjacked" it on the spot because it's terrific!)

You need:
- 1 package (2-layer size) sour cream chocolate cake mix
- 2 cups prepared Dream Whip or whipping cream
- 1 4-ounce jar of maraschino cherries, chopped
- 1/2 cup chopped walnuts

With love: Bake cake mix as box directs in two 8" layer cake tins—greased, floured, and with waxed paper. After cake has baked AND cooled, split layers to make 4 round layers, or 2 rectangular layers. Spread half or more of the Dream Whip (or whipped cream) on layers. Save enough for the top. Do NOT frost the cake sides. Sprinkle chopped cherries and walnuts over Dream Whip. Place other layer on top and spread Dream Whip, cherries and walnuts. Keep this stored in the refrigerator.

Coconut Lemon Surprise

You need:
- 1 package (2-layer size) lemon cake mix
- 1 3/4-ounce package instant lemon pudding
- 3 1/2-oz. can shredded (or flaked) coconut
- 1 package whipped white frosting mix (7-minute type)

With love: Bake cake as box directs in a greased, floured and waxed papered 9" by 13" baking pan. (Grease the pan with butter, then sprinkle a small amount of flour over it, shaking the pan to cover bottom and sides. Cut sheet of waxed paper to fit bottom of pan and place cake batter over it.) Mix instant pudding as box directs in small bowl and refrigerate until ready to use. After cake has cooled, remove it from pan and split the layer. Spread pudding on bottom layer and top with other layer. Mix whipped frosting as box directs and frost sides and top of cake. Sprinkle lavishly with coconut.

Serves 10

Now, here are some "from scratch" cakes.

Old-Fashioned Oatmeal Cake

You need: 1 1/4 cups boiling water
　　　　 1 cup QUICK oatmeal
　　　　 1/2 cup butter or margarine
　　　　 1 cup white sugar
　　　　 1 cup brown sugar
　　　　 2 eggs
　　　　 1 teaspoon cinnamon
　　　　 1 teaspoon vanilla
　　1 1/3 cups sifted flour
　　　　 1 teaspoon soda

With love: Pour boiling water over oatmeal and let stand 20 minutes or while you cream butter and sugars together. Add eggs, cinnamon, vanilla. Mix well. Then add oatmeal, flour, and soda. Mix and pour into a 9″ by 13″ baking pan. Bake 30 minutes at 350°.

Serves 6-8

This cake stays moist and good for days, if it's not eaten up first. If you serve it while it's still warm, it doesn't need frosting. If you have any of those pretty party doilies, put one layer of them on top of the warm cake and sprinkle powdered sugar over it. Carefully lift the doilies straight off and your white powdered sugar will have left a pretty design.

If you MUST frost this cake, use this butter frosting recipe and add two DROPS of maple flavoring.

Butter Creme Delight

You need: 1/2 cup butter (or one stick—1/4 pound)
　　　　 4 cups SIFTED powdered sugar
　　　　 1 egg yolk (if you have it)
　　1 1/2 teaspoons vanilla
　　　　 2 tablespoons of milk
　　　　 (2 drops maple flavoring for oatmeal cake)

With love: Cream butter and add about 2 cups powdered sugar. Add egg yolk and vanilla. Slowly add remaining sugar. Slowly add milk last. You may not want to use both tablespoons. Add maple flavoring. Frosting should be spreading consistency.

Your mother gave me these two cake recipes. They are simply delicious.

Easygoing Cake

You need:　1 16-ounce can fruit cocktail (undrained)
　　　　　1 cup sugar
　　　　　1 cup flour
　　　　　1 teaspoon soda
　　　　　1 pinch salt
　　　　　1 egg

Topping: 1/2 cup brown sugar
　　　　　1/4 teaspoon cinnamon
　　　　　1/4 cup chopped walnuts

With love: Combine first six ingredients and mix until smooth. Pour into 9″ by 13″ baking pan. Make topping and sprinkle on top. Bake for 45 minutes at 350° (top should be slightly brown).

Your Mom's Carrot Cake

You need:
- 2 cups sugar
- 1 1/2 cups vegetable oil (less 2 tablespoons)
- 4 eggs
- 1 1/2 teaspoons vanilla
- 2 1/2 cups flour (use self-rising if you have it)
- 1 teaspoon baking soda
- 2 teaspoons cinnamon
- 3 cups grated carrots

With love: Mix in a large bowl sugar, oil, eggs and vanilla for about 2 minutes. Gradually add flour, soda and cinnamon. Fold in carrots last. This will be a lot of batter and you will use 3 or 4 cake pans. Grease *and* flour pans. Bake for 30 min. at 350°.

This cake was made for a cream cheese frosting, so here is a great one.

Cheese Frost

You need:
- 1 3-oz. package cream cheese (softened)
- 4 tablespoons butter or margarine
- 1 teaspoon vanilla a dash of salt
- 2 1/2 cups sifted powdered sugar
- 1/2 cup chopped walnuts or pecans

With love: Cream cheese and butter. Beat in vanilla and salt. Slowly add sugar, mix well. Stir in nuts. Frost cake.

"As American as Mom and apple pie," the saying goes, and it's no accident about the pie bit. Pies seem to be the most favored American dessert. When you have an afternoon, a good bake oven, and a yen to make a pie, take down your big cookbook and start with "the crust" recipe and go to it.

If in 20 years of marriage you can whip and roll out a flaky, tender pie crust, you will have something to crow about. However, in the meantime, the packaged pie crust mix will do.

I say this to you because after several years of trying I *can* make a tender, flaky pie crust from scratch that turns out great —but not always. So I've found the mix is a little *less* delicious and a little *more* dependable. Of course, the best idea yet is to have a pie with a cracker crust or none at all. Here are Phyllis White's blueberries again, but this time it's a delicious pie.

Blueberry Ice Box Pie

You need *for crust*:
- 2 cups crushed cinnamon crisp graham crackers
- 1/2 cup melted butter or margarine

filling:
- 1 8-oz. package cream cheese (softened)
- 1 cup powdered sugar
- 1 cup chopped pecans or walnuts
- 1 package prepared Dream Whip or 1 cup whipped cream

topping:
- 1 16-oz. can blueberry pie filling

crust: Mix crushed crackers and butter together. Press into a 9″ pie pan. Chill in fridge.

filling: Mix cheese, powdered sugar, nuts, and Dream Whip. Pour filling into pie crust and chill.

topping: After chilling pie 15 or 20 minutes, spread blueberry pie filling mix on top. (You could use any pie filling mix. Cherry pie filling looks beautiful for Christmas, Valentine's Day, or 4th of July! But BLUEBERRY is extra special.) Keep refrigerated.

Serves 6-8

I never see those green pippin apples in the market without thinking of a dear lady named Mrs. Holmes. She was born in New Zealand and was a professional cook. She never gave away any of her recipes, but one night I asked her to give me a simple one to remember her by. She threw caution to the wind and whispered this, her own creation, to me. Both she and her husband have died and gone on to be with the Lord, but when I see apples I do love remembering her.

Mom Holmes' Apple Bake

You need: 1 2-crust package pie crust mix
5-9 (depending on size) peeled and thinly sliced green apples
1/2 cup white sugar
1/2 cup brown sugar
1/2 teaspoon cinnamon
1/4 teaspoon nutmeg
butter
1 MORE cup brown sugar
1 cup cold water

With love: Line an 8″ by 12″ baking pan with one stick prepared pie crust mix. Fill with sliced apples. Sprinkle with white and brown sugar, cinnamon, and nutmeg. Dot whole thing with butter. Cover with another stick of prepared pie crust mix and pinch and seal edges together. Nothing fancy, just tuck under here and there. Dot the top with butter.

All of this is pretty standard procedure up to this point, but here's her little trick which tells you (after you've tasted it) why she was good at her trade.

Sprinkle one MORE cup brown sugar over the top crust and then gently pour one cup cold water over the whole thing.

Bake one hour at 350°. The sugar and water on top makes a warm, bubbly sauce over the whole business and its fragrance spells pure L-O-V-E.

One-Bowl Brownie Pie

You need: 2 eggs
1 cup sugar
1/2 cup butter or margarine (softened)
1/2 cup flour
3 tablespoons cocoa
1 teaspoon vanilla
1/4 teaspoon salt
1/2 cup chopped walnuts

With love: You dump—and I do mean dump— all the ingredients except nuts into one bowl. Beat it with a mixer (or by hand) for 4 minutes. Add nuts and pour into an 8" or 9" pie pan. Bake 30 minutes at 350°. The pie will settle down in the middle as it cools. (That's all right, it doesn't hurt the taste.) Cut in wedges and serve with a topping of whipped cream or a la mode with a scoop of ice cream.

Serves 6

These next recipes are desserts which are simple, delicious, and not NECESSARILY fattening. The first one has a title longer than it takes to make, but it's great.

Petits Pats de Creme au Chocolat

You need: 1 3 3/4-oz. package of chocolate fudge pudding
2 cups milk (or half & half if you have it)
1 egg yolk
1 oz. semisweet chocolate (grated) OR 1/4 cup Nestle's Toll House Morsels
1/4 cup chopped pecans
1/2 cup whipped cream (or Dream Whip)

With love: Cook pudding as box directs with milk and add egg yolk. Add chocolate at the last minute. The chocolate does not have to completely melt. Pour into little china "pots" (if you have them), custard cups, or small sherbet dishes. Top with whipped cream and sprinkling of nuts.

Serves 4

Crispy Apple Dish

You need
for the filling: 1 can (1-pound, 9-ounce) apple pie filling mix

topping: 1/2 cup butter
1/2 cup brown sugar
1/2 cup unsifted flour
1/2 cup quick oatmeal

With love: Place apple filling in a greased 9" by 9" square baking dish. In a small pan melt butter and add brown sugar, flour, and oatmeal. Crumble this mixture on top of apple pie filling. Bake uncovered for 50 minutes at 350°.

You can use this next apple recipe as a dessert if you want to, but it could also double as a side dish to baked pork chops or ham.

Delicious Sliced Apples

You need: 6 cups thinly sliced green (pippin) apples
2 tablespoons chopped walnuts
2 tablespoons raisins
3/4 cup brown sugar
1/2 cup honey
1 cup water

With love: Place apple slices in an 8" by 12" rectangular baking dish. In a small bowl combine walnuts, raisins, and only 1/4 cup of the brown sugar. Sprinkle over the apples. In a small pan combine honey, water, and rest of the brown sugar (1/2 cup). Bring to boil and stir until sugar dissolves. Boil for 3 or 4 more minutes. Pour over apples. Bake uncovered 35 minutes at 350° (or until apples are tender). They are good warm or cold.

Makes 6-8 servings

When our children (your husband) were small, our friends, Ruth and Eleanor, sent them a jello dessert. (I can't recall the occasion, just the dessert.) We have continued to serve it for years now and it's still a refreshing treat especially in the summer.

Pink Cloud

You need:　1 6-oz. package any red jello (strawberry or cherry)
1 cup prepared Dream Whip or whipping cream
2 sliced bananas

With love: Make jello as box directs in a deep bowl. Refrigerate and let set. Make Dream Whip (or whipping cream). When jello is set, use your electric mixer to beat until jello is frothy. Then add cream and bananas and whip just until mixed. Spoon into individual sherbet glasses or pretty bowls. Return to the refrigerator to set.

Serves 4-6

If you want something sweet, light, and delicious at breakfast time, try either one of these next two recipes.

Excellent Banana Bread

You need:　3 ripe or overripe bananas (4 if small)
1 cup sugar
1 egg
1 1/2 cups flour
1/4 cup melted butter
1 teaspoon baking soda
1 teaspoon salt
1/2 cup chopped walnuts

With love: Mash bananas with fork. Stir in other ingredients. Pour into Teflon or buttered 8 1/2 by 4 1/2 by 2 1/2" loaf pan. Bake 1 hour in preheated 325° oven.

Selma's Coffee Cake

You need: 1/2 cup butter (or one stick)
1 cup sugar
2 eggs
2 cups flour
1 teaspoon soda
1 teaspoon baking powder
1/2 teaspoon salt
1 cup sour cream
Topping: 3/4 cup brown sugar
1/2 cup white sugar
2 teaspoons cinnamon
1/2 cup chopped walnuts (if you have them)

With love: Cream butter and sugar together in a large bowl. Add all the rest of ingredients (except topping stuff, of course). Mix and pour into greased

9″ by 13″ baking pan. Then mix all ingredients of the topping together and sprinkle over the cake batter, covering whole top. Then gently cut through the batter with a knife. You can make little swirls or line designs or what-have-you, but this puts some of that good topping down under. Bake uncovered 40 minutes at 325°.

Serves 8

To end this dessert chapter, I'll include two of the best cookie recipes I've ever made. For many Christmasses I've knocked myself out making all those fancy, frosted, jellied, intricate cookies only to hear everyone ask, "Where are those little white ones?" So, a few years ago I gave up on those others and just concentrated on "those little white ones."

Those Little White Ones

(cookies)

You need: 1 cup butter (do NOT substitute margarine here, it DOES make a difference)
4 tablespoons sugar
1 cup whole almonds
2 cups flour
1 box powdered sugar

With love: Cream butter and sugar. If you have a blender, pulverize the one cup of almonds. (If you don't have one, chop almonds fine.) Add ground (or chopped) almonds to butter and sugar, and mix. Add and mix flour into dough a little at a time in about

3 portions. Now, this next part is not tricky, just time-consuming. Shape the dough into 10″ or 12″ long rolls, making the diameter of the roll the size of a 25¢ piece. Place rolls on flat cookie sheets, cover with plastic wrap and refrigerate for a few hours or overnight. After they have completely chilled, slice the long rolls into cookie rounds 1/8″ thick (if you can't get them that thin, go to 1/4″ thick, but try for thin-thin). Bake on an ungreased cookie sheet 40 minutes at 275°. While they are baking, sift powdered sugar into a paper bag. When cookies are baked and STILL WARM, drop them (a few at a time) into the bag of sugar to be coated. Let them "dry" on metal cake racks. These freeze well for later use so you COULD start your Christmas cookies in October if you wanted to.

Lila's Cherry and Coconut Bars

You need
for bottom layer: 1 cup sifted flour
1/2 cup butter (or margarine)
3 tablespoons powdered sugar
Topping: 2 slightly beaten eggs
1 cup sugar
1/4 cup flour
1/2 teaspoon baking powder
1/4 teaspoon salt
1 teaspoon vanilla
1/2 cup chopped walnuts
1/2 cup shredded or flaked coconut
1/2 cup quartered maraschino cherries

With love: Heat your oven to 350°. Then use your hands to mix flour, butter, and sugar until smooth. Spread and pat down in a 9″ square pan. Bake 25 minutes at 350°.

While that's baking, mix the topping ingredients and as soon as the bottom layer is baked, spread topping over it (no need to cool it). Bake the whole thing for 25 minutes more. (Near the 20-minute mark you want to peek at it as it burns easily.) Completely cool and THEN cut into bars or squares.

Just think, you have a whole marriage ahead of you to develop not only these recipes but other dessert goodies as well! I'm looking forward to the day you phone me and say, *"Boy, have I got a recipe for you!"*

CHAPTER SEVEN
Flowers and Candlelight

A famous psychiatrist once said, "Tell me in detail what your evening dinner hour is like and I'll tell you about your family relationships." That should give you a fair idea of how important the dinner hour is.

We tend to think that everyone's dinner time is just like the one we are accustomed to. If we have had lots of infighting and bickering at the table, we think that's normal. If we have had meat, potatoes, and NO vegetables or salads, we think that's the only way to eat. If we've had a centerpiece of flowers and candles every dinner hour, we think that's the way it is with all families' dinner hour.

But in talking with many people and teaching a creative cooking class to Azusa Pacific College students I've learned a whole lot about dinner hours.

In the first place, EVERYONE has a different experience to share. Whenever I've asked if the memory of eating together in their home was a happy or a painful one, I've been astounded with the answers. Nine out of ten said it was rather painful. Here are some examples: Some families never have a time when they all sit together for one meal (dinner, lunch, or breakfast). Some gather silently, gulp all food down as fast as possible, and without conversation, disappear with the last mouthful. Still others collect at the end of the day to have dinner and one long fight. Many families have highly UNbalanced meals (all starchy foods or meat and potatoes with no vegetables or greens of any kind). Some families use the dinner hour to discuss (critically) people and problems. RARE is the family who comes to the dinner table hungry for food and fellowship and leaves richly satisfied in both areas.

This last dinner hour is what I would pray for you to have. It won't be easy; and will require a meeting of minds between you and your husband. It will take time and effort on your part, but you are about to build a tower of memories and at this point in your life you can decide whether those memories will be happy or painful.

Guidelines for Dinner

Here are some guidelines for the every night meal at your house.

1. Set a pleasant, warm table.

The first time I realized our dinner hour was blah, I found a bare, unattractive setting as well as the shape of the table could (and DID!) influence our dinner hour with the same unattractive BLAHS!

I don't know who invented the long breakfast bar or counter for eating, but whoever it was probably had an unhappy childhood. There is NOTHING so unconducive to eating, sharing, passing food or seeing one another as sitting (lined up like so many pigeons at a shooting gallery) at a counter.

I moved our family from the counter to the oval dining room table (the one I'd saved for "company only"). Then I took a good look at the table top itself.

As I stood there looking at it, I remembered something my mother told me many years before. She had been ironing twice a week for a wealthy lady in Pasadena so she could afford to have me take voice lessons. It was one of those beautiful things she did for me when I was a teenager. She did it though with absolutely no trace of poor-me-I-work-so-hard-and-sacrifice-so-much. Naturally, her great attitude turned the whole experience into a grand learning adventure.

One day as we drove home from her regular day of ironing, she told me what the lady of the house had done at lunchtime. My mother said she would always use the ideas she had learned that day (and she did).

The lady of the house had taken my mother's brown sack lunch and disappeared with it. When noon rolled around, my mother was ushered into the grand dining room and there, all by itself on a highly polished, magnificent table, was Mother's lunch.

The linen placemat and napkin were beautiful. The whole wheat bread and peanut butter sandwich and celery sticks were arranged on a china plate. In front of the placemat was one lovely rose in a crystal vase. As she sat my mother down the lady said, "Now, my dear, whenever you eat, whether it's with your family or completely alone, set a pleasant, warm table. Use the best of what you have and it will help you to lay down the cares of this world so you can enjoy and fully appreciate eating and being alive."

Setting a pleasant, warm table begins by bringing your family AROUND a table. Then use placemats for everyday and tablecloths for special times. Finally, complete the table picture by using a centerpiece of flowers, fruit, or some fun decoration and candles.

The first time I made a centerpiece of three or four flowers from our yard and lit two candles at dinner time I took quite a ribbing. I'll never forget it!

First, my husband made all kinds of cracks like, "Why is it so dark in here? Is the food so bad that we are trying to cover it up?" Then both he and our son decided maybe the food DID look better that night by candlelight. Later, while I was having a fun fit, they got hysterical with laughter as they decided not only did the food definitely look better by candlelight, but I did, TOO!

Long after dinner that night, and in the privacy of our bedroom, I talked with my husband. I told him how fun dinner had been, but that I *was serious* about flowers and candlelight. I felt it was our only time to be together as a family. It was our only time to talk to each other, to find out how it was going in everyone's world and to share a bit of ourselves with each other. I wanted it to be a happy, warm time and I asked my husband if he would share the responsibility with me in making great memories for us and our children. I think, at that point, he didn't think flowers and candlelight made *that* much difference, but he was a great sport and said he'd back me all the way. (BLESS him!!)

Quite often when someone stops by during our dinner they always see our table, and say, "Oh, I'm sorry, I didn't know you were having a special party tonight." My husband always beams with that special smile of his and says, "No, no special party. This is standard procedure for every dinner hour at our house." It's a beautiful time for all of us and our hearts will always hold these treasured memories.

2. Cook something new at least once a week.

Never limit your meals to just CERTAIN things. That's as bad as having to stick to a rigid, restricted diet. Be adventuresome with your cooking. It helps to develop and broaden your tastes. Some foods (like artichokes and avocados) take time to acquire a taste for, but given in small amounts from time to time you can learn to appreciate them.

3. Structure the dinner conversation towards fun and information.

Some dinner conversations are nonexistent. When that happens it is usually because a person has grown up in a home where nobody said anything during dinner. That person will need help in breaking a lifelong habit and will find it hard to talk. But it can be done. You can begin by talking about any subject: weather, job, sports happenings, historical, or current events, etc.

When our children were young we asked, "What was the happiest thing that happened to you today?" Other times when we asked, "What was the WORST thing about today?" we got some pretty lively dinner discussions. When they reached high school they spent a good deal of the dinner hour on all the latest teen-age jokes (funny, funny!).

Try to avoid accusative conversation. Don't waste effort, time, or digestion by discussing the problematic areas of your

life. Don't discipline your children at the table over the bike they left out in the rain (it rusted) or their room (which looks like a disaster area). AFTER dinner is soon enough to talk about it and to take disciplinary action.

To help structure conversation, shut *off* the television and turn on some dinner music. We always had a radio station turned on—very low—to semiclassical music during dinner. Without their knowing it, we gave our children a music appreciation course for "our kind" of music, done very slyly at dinner time.

4. Teach each person how to appreciate one another.

People have always asked us how we managed to have such beautifully polite children. After our stock, glib answer of, "We beat them twice a week," we usually said, "We TAUGHT them, both by example and by lecturing."

Most of us are not *naturally* born to the art of appreciating things and being kind to people. We must be taught and we must learn it.

Your husband should be thanked for earning the money to buy the food for your table.

You should be thanked for shopping for it, storing it, cooking it and serving it.

Your children (when they are old enough) should be thanked for helping in setting the table or clearing the dishes or cleaning up afterward. By the way, when your children are babies, those strained carrots will go down much better with your loving encouragement!

During our dinner prayer I have been known to interrupt or add, "And bless the loving hands that prepared this food," if I thought the person praying would not be using that phrase.

Ending dinner with all of us thanking each other for the success of the meal has made us a happy, warm family and certainly *hasn't* hindered our digestion in the process.

Etiquette is not a dirty nine-lettered word, but its meaning has been highly maligned and twisted. Etiquette does NOT mean rigid rules, sissy techniques, or impossible guidelines. It means simply BEING KIND TO EACH OTHER!

One of the secondary themes of the New Testament seems to me to be this very doctrine. "And whatever you do, do it with kindness and love" (1 Cor. 16:14 TLB).

So if we boil the words ETIQUETTE and MANNERS down to being kind, then,

> If you chew with your mouth closed—you are BEING kind.

> If your husband helps to seat you first and then your children or guests—he is PRACTICING, in a physical way, kindness.

> If you leave the table to blow your nose a good one—you are considering others and BEING kind.

> If you put into actual words your appreciation for the meal—you are verbally SHOWING kindness.

If you concentrate on drawing conversations and laughter out of your family during dinner—you are helping to build terrific memories and that is the kindest act of all!

These are only a few suggestions for manners, but they add up in our learning to appreciate each other.

Now, I'd like to list some guidelines for you as you entertain guests in your home. Besides being kind, we are told in the New Testament to be hospitable and here are some practical helps to get you started in that direction

1. Keep a simple record.

I wish for all the years we have been married I'd have kept a record of dinners, people and menus. You tend to forget and all the details fuse and blend together over the years. I hope it won't happen to you. Since it's never too late to learn, I've started my own card collection!

In the back of a recipe box keep a section marked "GUESTS." Then make out several 3" by 5" cards like this:

Name of dinner occasion:		Date:	
Guest list:		Beverage	Menu
What you wore and any			Table
special idea used in			centerpiece
entertaining:			used:

It only takes a second or two to fill out a card, but it can be of great assistance to you in planning for guests or family.

Under the "beverages" column make up your own code for whether your guest is a coffee or tea drinker and what they use in it. (Those who like coffee black could be listed as "C. blk." or for tea with lemon, "T.w.lem." or just "W" for water only.) No one needs to know you keep a record, but I'll guarantee when a guest returns to your house and you say, "Now, let's see, you have coffee black and your wife has tea with lemon," your hospitality will NEVER be forgotten.

By checking your records you will be reminded of what you served, when and to whom, and duplications are avoided.

This little 3" by 5" card system is one of the most helpful ways to be a gracious hostess. It speaks loudly of your ability to *really* care for people in your own home. That brings me to the next point.

2. Put the care and feeding of guests on the top of your priority list.

You see, Honey, you don't have to have a Home Ec. degree in cooking to make your entertaining special, but you do have to have a large degree in CARING.

See to the needs of your guests by serving them first, watching to refill their cup of coffee or their water glass and ANTICIPATING their extra needs *before* they ask for the salt or butter.

Just observe and practice the simple and kind rules of etiquette. You will NOT be a perfect hostess overnight, but even in your earliest entertaining you can gain experience and knowledge. Make those failures or bad moments work for you. When you have successes look them over, see why they were good, and try to repeat them.

3. Cook what is familiar to you.

Trying out a new recipe on guests is a little like finding out company is going to drop by in ten minutes. We are *highly motivated* to clean the entire house in one full swoop, but because of tension and strain NOTHING seems to go right. So don't be tempted to cook something special or fancy because company is coming. Save that idea for some dull Wednesday night. Then if it flops the percentage of people who witness it is considerably lower and you'll know not to try THAT one again.

4. You and your husband greet guests at or near the front door.

This isn't always too easy, but it's important. First impressions are very strong and hard to erase. You may be involved at a crucial time at the stove, but try to arrange it so you can be at the door. This is true even with best friends and relatives—a welcome is essential to anyone who enters your home. (Incidentally, never underestimate the warmth of a welcome when there is no company around—just the two of you. We love to be greeted when we come home, no matter how long or short the time away has been. Like our little dog Sydney; he has no wrist watch so is not aware if we've been gone five days or five minutes. But his welcome is always the same—PURE JOY AT SEEING US.

5. You and your husband are just as responsible for the food (and serving it) as you are for the fun and conversation.

Keep conversation alive and the food available for a great time.

Well, my darling Daughter-In-Law, (or daughter-in-LOVE, as I prefer), I've probably left out some important hints or recipes, but there is enough here to get you off to a good start.

Before I close this book, there is one more thing I want to share with you. I'm sure you are not aware that I've kept every little note from you—even the ones you wrote before you were married. I think it's important here to include some excerpts from them.

Once, in a thank you note to me about a bridal shower gift you said,

"Dearest Joyce,

Yesterday was a very special day for me and Rick.... Oh, Joyce, the shower was so beautiful.

When Rick and I put away our 'new' things I was so proud. Once the things were all in place Rick shared about a prayer time he'd spent with our Lord thanking him for ALL we have. Joyce, it was so neat because he stopped, looked at me and said, 'Oh, Teresa, we have so much to be thankful for!' And it's true! We have you to thank for so much of what we have. Not just our material gifts but for the precious moments you've shared with us teaching, guiding, and having us learn about the love of our God—and what a marriage centered on Him should be.

My dear Mother-In-Love-to-be, God couldn't have given me a better one."

Then later, Darling Daughter-in-Love, you were so wonderful to write my husband of your love, do you remember? You said,

"Dick, not only is Joyce going to make the best mother-in-love, but you will make the greatest father-in-love! I really love you. The Lord couldn't have picked in-laws that would be more special to me than you two.

Thank you for raising Rick the way you have. You and Joyce have raised a terrific man of God. And I love him with all my heart. Rick is just like you, Dick, and someday he'll make the same great daddy to our children as you have been to Rick. Thank you!"

Later, you wrote this special note of thanks to me.

"I love you, Joyce. Thank you for praying for me before I ever met Rick."

But the note that really sent my heart flying into the clouds was the one that ended with.

"Oh, Joyce, I love you and you're going to make
the greatest,
the most fantastic,
beautiful, and
classy
mother-in-love in the whole world!"

Oh, Teresa—I pray so! I pray so!

Hang in there, Darling Daughter-in-Love and remember . . . always

MIX BUTTER WITH LOVE!

Acknowledgements

This book comes to you because of a considerable number of mothers-in-law who are terrific cooks and willing to share their recipes.

It also comes to you because of the outside-the-kitchen talents of Brenda Arnold and Sheila Rapp who corrected and typed; of Bob Hawkins and staff, who worked diligently on this manuscript and always showered me with encouragement; and last but not least, dear Francis Hook who, with her pen lifted from dry, ordinary words, drawings fragrant with butter and love!

I thank them all!

Joyce Landorf